MW00857090

"In *Liquid Luck*, clinical | practical guide to operating from love rather tulates that any of us might begin our journey 'to become [the] conscious creator of one's reality' by insisting that we be fully present in the moment, and through a series of clearly delineated exercises, embrace gratitude, abundance, compassion, and the like. *Liquid Luck* may lead some to material gain. yet has the potential to teach many how to let go of negativity, manifest joy, and become conduits of change in our communities."

—Amit Goswami, Ph.D., author of *Quantum Creativity:*
Think Quantum, Be Creative

"I read the *Liquid Luck* handbook, then listened to both the *Liquid Luck* CD and the *Abundance Waterfall* CD. And . . . *every single expert* I reached out to was willing to speak with me! From book authors and scientists with articles in peer-reviewed journals, to the head of a research institute. Honestly, it has been amazing, and I am truly grateful for the contributions these people have made to my articles."

—Nancy Nelson, Founder of *More Than Passing Strange* e/magazine

"If you're looking for a fun, easy, and effective way to attract what you want in life, make sure you read this book! In an engaging and inviting style, Dr. Joe Gallenberger clearly explains his 'Liquid Luck' approach for achieving your dreams. I've seen Joe's techniques work time and again with participants he has trained at the MC² programs at The Monroe Institute. In fact, after reading just the first 50 pages of this book, not only was I inspired by the stories of others' success and the simple yet profound concepts Joe shares for manifesting, the next morning I was delighted to be given one of the largest donations the Institute has ever received! *Liquid Luck: The Good Fortune Handbook* is a must-read for anyone wanting to make positive and phenomenal changes in their lives!"

—Nancy H. McMoneagle, president and executive director,
The Monroe Institute

"There are lots of prosperity/create-your-own-reality books on the market. What makes *Liquid Luck* different is that it is a complete system for reprogramming emotions and behavior and for redirecting energetic vibrations in order to achieve more effective results in the physical world—and the physical world is where Gallenberger begins. The book starts with the basics of grounding in happiness, then moves on to in-depth explanations for enhancing and practicing gratitude, abundance, compassion, love, and praise. The last part of the book gives readers specific ways for dealing with the challenges and resistance that naturally arise during the process of change. Let customers know that Gallenberger has CDs/downloads available on his website that will help them put the information in the book into practice. The book by itself does, however, give readers all the basics for taking their lives into their own hands in order to make changes that will increase their sense of well-being. It is a dynamic resource for those who want to learn to make miracles, even if they don't believe it's possible."

—Anna Jedrziewski, *Retailing Insight* (formerly *New Age Retailer*)

"In *Liquid Luck*, Dr. Gallenberger outlines the well-researched and successful Hemisphere-Synchronization process designed by Bob Monroe of the Monroe Institute to facilitate rapid and deep shifts in consciousness, allowing for new creativity and energy to be applied to the creation of luck and abundance. Dr. Gallenberger takes the reader through a series of specific guided meditations on gratitude, abundance, compassion, loving awareness, praise, and luck. He then explains how binaural beats actually work to synchronize the two hemispheres of the brain in order to produce a more expanded state of awareness during these guided meditations. *Liquid Luck* presents one of the most practical applications of the meditation process I've come across in many years."

—Reviewed by Matthew Miller, The Institute for Global Transformation

Liquid
LUCK

The Good Fortune Handbook

JOSEPH GALLENBERGER, Ph.D.

RAINBOW RIDGE
BOOKS

Cover and interior design by Frame25 Productions
Cover photo © Weeraphon Suriwongsa c/o Shutterstock.com

Published by:
Rainbow Ridge Books, LLC
1056 Commodore Drive
Virginia Beach, VA 23454
www.rainbowridgebooks.com

If you are unable to order this book from your local
bookseller, you may order directly from the distributor.

Square One Publishers, Inc.
115 Herricks Road
Garden City Park, NY 11040
877-900-BOOK

Visit the author at:
www.SyncCreation.com
www.LiquidLuckbook.com

Library of Congress Cataloging-in-Publication Data applied for.

ISBN 978-1-937907-27-3

10 9 8 7 6 5 4

Printed in India through Nutech Print Services

To my wife Elena, my true "Anam Cara":
soul mate, friend, business partner,
and fellow traveler on the abundance road.

ACKNOWLEDGEMENTS

I thank my wife Elena for the good cheer and support both at home and on the road, and keeping our family and business going while I was writing this book. My appreciation is extended to Robert Friedman, president of Rainbow Ridge Books for encouraging this project, editing, and bringing it to publication. I am filled with gratitude for all the participants who have been to my workshops, inspiring me with their love and courage as they explore the limits of consciousness. And I want to acknowledge the people who have experienced the Liquid Luck CD/download and taken the time to write me about their manifestation victories. They inspired this project and without their stories this book would not have been written.

CONTENTS

INTRODUCTION

The first day I tried Liquid Luck, we solved a complex hardware/software interface problem in the lab that had resisted our efforts for two years. Not bad! I liked the format, very smooth. Will use it again, and let you know what else happens. Thanks. —R.D.

In the past year I developed a meditation exercise designed to summarize decades of experience teaching manifestation into its essential components. This exercise can be applied effectively in less than one hour's time. The idea was for the exercise to provide the listener with an exceptionally lucky day filled with wisdom, synchronicity, and good fortune whenever desired. Within hours of its release on compact disc, as *Liquid Luck: A Heart Based Meditation Designed to Increase Good Fortune,* stories of success began flooding in. I will share many of these stories as we journey through this book. The meditation was constructed to slip under the formidable emotional and belief blocks that usually frustrate attempts to improve our situations and to facilitate immediate access to the special energies needed to create what we desire quickly and easily.

As time went on the amazing stories of success continued. People were having results in areas that I had not anticipated, well beyond increased financial abundance. It became clear to me that a book that explored more deeply why the Liquid Luck meditation is so effective and elaborated on the special, even sacred, energies triggered by the meditation would be most helpful. The book will include many exercises and tips for generating and sustaining these important manifestation energies.

While *Liquid Luck*, the meditation, was designed to trigger an exceptionally lucky day, *Liquid Luck*, the book reveals why this works and how these same principles applied more broadly every day, can result in a life filled to the brim with abundance, love, and happiness. This state of continuous well-being can benefit the reader, loved ones, and the larger community in significant ways. As with the meditation, I am committed to making this book as clear, concise, and practical as possible.

My book, *Inner Vegas: Creating Miracles, Abundance and Health*, describes in detail my journey of discovery and application of energy to influence physical reality in my own life and then with my students. I will summarize *Inner Vegas* here in a few paragraphs so that you have some idea where I am coming from up to the point where *Liquid Luck* begins.

I am a clinical psychologist with thirty years experience as a therapist. I retired from clinical practice about nine years ago to devote my time to teaching how to enhance what we manifest into our lives. In 1992, I began to investigate psychokinesis (PK), which is the ability to influence matter through non-physical means. PK can be used to illuminate light bulbs, bend metal and plastic, sprout seeds in your hand, influence computers, dice, and slot machines, and create healing and abundance—all just using the power of your human energy in a special way. Being able to do these things is incredibly exciting to me! Another great thing about PK is that it can be measured scientifically and results can be shown, often in minutes, giving ultra clear feedback that "something important is happening."

Achieving powerful PK results to a high degree of statistical significance at a university laboratory under controlled conditions allowed me to know that PK was real. The experiments gave me a taste of how the wonderful the energy needed to do PK felt. As I was applying PK and seeing results, my heart would often be pounding. I felt surges of joy, gratitude, and amazement.

After five years of developing methods to convey this skill to groups, I have used my discoveries to host over seventy *Inner Vegas Adventure*™ workshops in the casinos of Las Vegas, where participants journey deeply into personal power. My students often achieve dramatic physical and psychological healing, strong influence over dice and slot machines, and many marvelous manifestations in their lives at home. The casino is an excellent classroom because in using PK to manifest abundance there, with the concrete feedback of win and loss, it is clear within minutes whether the person is being effective at the principles being taught. And with even small amounts of money being wagered, motivation and attention to the lessons is very high! This allows very rapid learning of the mental and emotional field and skill set required for the most effective manifesting of what one desires.

When some people see or hear the word Vegas, they immediately respond, "Oh, this is not for me, I don't gamble." Well, if you have ever married, had children, started a business, or even crossed the street in traffic, you are indeed a high roller, in that you are taking risks or gambling with things such as your health and happiness, which are much more important than money! To manifest abundance, it is helpful to embrace risk. Risk is good—it is how we learn, grow, and change things for the better. I can sympathize if your reaction to risk is leery. Most of us, including me, were taught that, "Oh, that is risky" meant caution, stop, do not proceed or you will hurt yourself or others. However, we would not have any new inventions, companies, marriage proposals, or progress if everyone avoided all risk. Would it not be better to learn how to risk intelligently, with clear access to the wisdom and intuition of your heart and surefire access to the correct energy to maximize chances of success? That is what is taught in my workshops.

I am also a senior facilitator at The Monroe Institute. I train a spectrum of Monroe programs and developed the Institute's highly successful MC² (Manifestation and Creation Squared) program which teaches psychokinesis, healing, and manifestation. I also developed SyncCreation® a Course in Manifestation, which is the home study version of the MC² program. I journey internationally as a workshop presenter on these topics.

The Monroe Institute (TMI) is world renowned as a place to explore the potentials of human consciousness using a special technology called Hemi-Sync®. This Hemi-Sync technology uses something called binaural beats, listened to over headphones that allow the listener to move easily into deep meditative states without years of practice. This deep meditation effect is achieved without need for any particular dogma. It works for atheists, Christians, Buddhists, Republicans, and Democrats alike.

My connection with the Monroe Institute is important to understand because part of the success of *Liquid Luck*, the recording, is because it uses a binaural beat technology similar to which I had been working with for over two decades at TMI. And this allows people listening to *Liquid Luck* to enter the enhanced states of awareness needed to easily and quickly tap into the special energies that I will be discussing in this book. For those interested I will go into more detail about this amazing technology and how it can help with abundance goals in Chapter Eleven of this book.

By the start of college I was familiar with books that discussed abundance creation including Norman Vincent Peale's *The Power of Positive Thinking*, first published in 1952; *Think and Grow Rich* by Napoleon Hill, first published in 1937; and Esther and Jerry Hicks *The Law of Attraction*, recently popularized by the film *The Secret*. In fact, these types of books go back at least to middle Egyptian dynasty times, in a work called the *Kabylion*. But for me all of this reading usually produced only weak or mixed results most of the time, until the study and practice of PK lit a fire under me by suggesting how to actually raise and focus the right kind of energy for miracle results.

It is fair to ask why this area of manifestation was and is so important to me.

On July 15, 1991 my dear brother Peter committed suicide. This rocked my world deeply. I wrote *Brother's Forever: An Unexpected Journey Beyond Death*, which was published in 1996 as a result of this experience. Peter was handsome, intelligent, honest, hard working, generous, and charismatic, yet he could not create success in work and after decades of effort slowly sunk into despair.

In my agonizing about the meaning of this event I began to ponder what happens when we don't positively influence our lives and, even worse, what happens if we tend to manifest the exact opposite of what we want on a regular basis—negative PK if you will! And what would cause a distortion in our life path such as chronic negative manifestation and all the suffering it produces for us and those around us? I realized fairly quickly that the main driver of such distortion was not a vengeful god but rather the playing out of the formidable energy of fear coupled with limiting beliefs. It does appear that we live in a free choice universe where we are free to think and feel negatively or positively. But the way we think and feel tends to become fairly habitual and when we do this consistently in one direction, that direction, whether negative or positive, begins to manifest and reinforce that particular direction, perpetuating the cycle be it negative or positive. It was clear from my brother's experience that it is not sufficient to be a good person; one must also feel deserving of receiving goodness, learn to alleviate fear, and to be in positive energy.

Catalyzed by my brother's death and often seeing similar patterns in my psychotherapy clients, I began to look at this more deeply. It seems that most people do little to actively influence their lives in a positive direction, except applying things such as study, hard work, and hope to goals that they would like to achieve . . . with a good bit of fear mixed in that they perhaps will not get the break, or are not good enough. That often results in a life with a mixture of good and bad things happening. There seems to be a continuum of those who seem to be naturally lucky people, to folks where most everything seems to go wrong. When we look more closely at each of the opposite ends of the spectrum, it becomes apparent that we are doing much to actively create our reality.

As in my brother's case, because of ever-increasing fear that he would not make it, in the context of mounting intolerable financial pressures, negative manifestation can result in disaster. On the other end of the continuum, we see ever-increasing success and we have the cultural wisdom, "the rich get richer." So we have some people who often unconsciously create horrendous situations for themselves, and those who create mostly richly rewarding experiences. Most people are hampered to a greater or lesser degree by their fears and lack of miracle energy, yet some people enjoy an ever-increasing arc of good fortune and often then bless the world with their abundance of ideas, money, job creation, and solutions to important problems. Yes, it is possible to make a great deal of money "on the backs of others," but this tends to come at a great personal cost in other important areas of abundance, such as happiness, health, nurturing relationships, and spiritual progress.

I feel it is very important to understand how we manifest our individual and collective lives, because at this time there is a high degree of fear in our world that is pulling us toward manifesting a very negative future. For example, because of fear of terrorism now, we see our privacy rights in the U.S. being diminished, where much of what we do is monitored and we can be taken without charges or legal representation to a unknown place for an unlimited time in the name of Homeland Security. So we have moved from the threat of terrorism taking away some our citizens' freedoms to live happily and healthy, to our fear response to terrorism, which indeed takes away the freedom, privacy, and important rights of all our citizens. This shift has been dramatic. When I traveled in Europe pre-9/11, there was a palpable appreciation and desire for the "American" way of life. Now when I travel there, folks respectfully take me aside and express concern that the American dream is dying in the United States. And many Europeans report their fear of coming to visit what they see now as the American police state, particularly if they have experienced firsthand the entry process for foreign visitors established at our borders after 9/11.

This saddens me deeply, but I also see the immense reserve of good will, creativity, and love of freedom that exists in the United States and know we can get back on track if we can get our fear under control. And that starts by the majority of us individually getting our own fear under control and visioning a positive future. Spoiler alert! I used to try to meet fear with courage, now I melt fear with love. And this book will give you many ways in invoke the power of love to do this. My new mantra is "Fear is expensive, love is priceless, choose wisely!" Someone was kind enough to put my saying on a wooden sign and gift it to me. I placed the sign on the wall of my office near my computer, where I see it many times a day. This is good because I need to be reminded of it often.

From my point of view we very much need to understand how we create our reality and master the tools needed for creating a positive future at this tipping point in our society. My hope is that this book will help many individuals create a much more heavenly situation for themselves, knowing that this is likely to positively impact those around them. But even further, as groups of people live from these empowering principles we can make rapid progress in creating a great future for the world community.

Chapter 1

HAPPINESS AND GROUNDING

I received the Liquid Luck CD Thursday afternoon. On Friday, I took the time to sit down and listen. When it was finished, I walked into the kitchen where I noted a flyer for my house magnetized to the refrigerator door. My home has been on the market since April 12. Circumstances have not been optimum for selling with a highway road construction project a block away. There are two other homes on my block for sale and my house hasn't had any viable interest in four months. I walked up to the flyer and put my hand on it and said, "I would like this sold." I kid you not. Within an hour, my realtor contacted me with an offer. After a couple of days of negotiations, the contract was ratified just about an hour ago. I wanted to wait until all the signatures were in before I told you about it. Thank you, Joe, for taking the time to do this. —P.A.

I would first like to talk about the core of the Liquid Luck meditation to introduce the special, sacred energies that in a deep meditative state are accessed during the exercise. We will be exploring each of these energies in detail as this book progresses because these energies, if lived daily, will create a miraculously fulfilling life.

In Liquid Luck, once the listener is relaxed, has off-loaded any limiting emotions and beliefs, and has raised their energy to a very high level in a manner that we will later discuss, here is the wording used about twelve minutes into the exercise. The words concerning happiness, the topic of this chapter, are in bold for emphasis.

"Within your expanded awareness and energy, in touch with more of who you truly are, you can create a new reality by imagining a new pattern vividly. This is the pattern we call Liquid Luck. Immerse yourself deeply into the experience. Experience the pattern as though it were already here, right in this very moment. Flowing in beautiful energy, design your pattern now, as I guide you.

Now imagine that you are a wizard or alchemist of considerable power and wisdom. Feel the comfortable and flowing garments that you are wearing, and look around at your familiar sanctuary where you study, practice, and expand your skills.

Today you are creating a wonderful new energy potion with very desirable and magical properties, called Liquid Luck. This potion, when swallowed, brings the drinker a day where everything fortuitously falls in place for great benefit. On this day—synchronicity, serendipity, grace, and positive energy abound, bringing you easily and joyfully to your highest good and desire. This potion brings the clarity to notice just the right thing at the right time . . . the impulse to move with just the right timing in the right direction . . . and the courage to act on these intuitions with great trust. This is an excellent potion to use whenever you desire help to achieve your goal . . . or even something better!

With great excitement you begin:

Imagine gently holding in front of you a small clear glass container that holds a sparkling liquid within. See this beautiful liquid swirling and sparkling before you . . . Now into this liquid you begin to send very high and special energies: **Say out loud or in your mind, "I am Happy" . . . feel happiness, and send this energy of happiness into your potion, the wonderful energy of a soaring spirit filled with joy.**

Then say, "I am Grateful" . . . feel gratitude and send gratitude, concentrating it into your elixir, thinking of all the wonderful blessings in your life and feeling your gratitude for them, and sending this energy into your potion.

Next say, "I am abundant" . . . feel abundant, and send the energy of abundance, remembering all the ways in which you are already highly abundant and sending this energy into your liquid.

Now say, "I am compassionate" . . . Feel your beauty, dignity, and sacredness, and your compassionate connection with all beings in their beauty—and send this energy of compassion into your potion

Say, "I am love" . . . feel love, and fill your container with the highest of love for yourself and all of creation.

Now let your heart expand further and join with spirit in joyful praising of all that is, say "I Praise All" . . . and send this praising energy into your elixir.

And now add the last magic ingredient. Say, "I am Lucky" and send all good fortune, synchronicity, and blessing into your potion.

Take a few more moments now, to complete your creation.
Now with your design complete . . . bless it with
great light, great love . . . and to the highest purpose for
your good and the good of all others. Gazing at your
container of Liquid Luck, say to yourself, "This creation
is my intention. So be it. So be it."

As you can see, the first energy introduced, the first energy to go into the vial, is happiness. Happiness opens us up to be receptive to new experiences. Can you recall a time when you were feeling blue, bored, or tired and someone suggested a new activity such as going to see a movie or play tennis? Usually we resist such a suggestion when in a funk. By contrast if we are feeling happy, we are more likely to say yes, look forward to the new activity and participate more fully, thereby increasing our enjoyment and happiness further.

Happiness is a very powerful state of mind. In fact, it is central to grounding, which is essential to powerful manifesting. It is almost impossible to create the life you desire without being grounded. So before we talk about how happiness affects grounding, let's explore grounding a bit further.

I emphasize grounding as an essential part of manifestation. At our deepest levels many of us are not one hundred percent sure whether we really want to be here in physical reality on planet Earth. This is understandable. There is a lot of pain, confusion, struggle, and darkness here. So we live slightly out-of-body, and disconnected from the present moment, flicking our attention between the past and the future to try to protect ourselves from pain. The impact of pain is dulled if we are not fully present. But if you wish to manifest your dreams into your life in a rapid, clear, and powerful way, you need to be fully here and present in your body. This is what we mean by being grounded. You are the anchor that pulls things in.

Many meditation systems serve to pull you up and away from physical life. This is great for relaxation and transcendence, but such connection to spirit needs to be integrated with grounding for effective manifestation. For example, we have learned that the most powerful healers, shamans, highly successful business persons, and athletes are very strongly grounded yet expanded in energy at the same time. Many books on manifestation fail to emphasize this and produce disappointing results. ***Grounding is a key secret to mastering positive creation.***

Being grounded is defined for our purposes as bringing your spirit *fully* into your body, suffusing the body with energy and light, allowing the physical and emotional body to speak to you without repression, appreciating your connection with the earth, and allowing its sacred energy into you—so that you are fully spirit and flesh at the same time, and your energies are focused in the present moment. This is your birthright—to be the "X" point bridging heaven and earth, body and spirit. And to me the center of the X is in your heart.

Many activities are naturally grounding. They include engaging in anything that is beautiful and pleasing to you about the physical world, such as: hot showers, sunsets, walks in nature, hugging a tree, basking in the sun, sitting with your feet in a stream, listening to music with a beat, dancing, physical exercise, tending a garden, body work, massage, and love-making. But the most important component is your own intention, your genuine desire to be fully here in the present moment. Grounding involves keeping in touch with what you love about the physical, and being willing to be here in each present moment.

Sometimes we experience unpleasant emotions or thoughts. It is important for grounding and long-term happiness not to deny or suppress these, but rather feel them, express them constructively, then let go and move on. If you are angry, express it and move one. If you need to grieve, do so fully and cleanly and move on. Holding a grudge and feeling like a victim pulls you out of the present moment and buries you in the past.

This is a positive feedback loop; the more you manifest what you desire in your life, emotionally and materially, the more you will want to be here. The more you want to be here, the more grounded you will tend to be, and the more easily you will manifest your dreams.

Make some form of grounding a daily exercise. I suggest at least fifteen minutes each morning and evening. I often take a short walk in the morning and evening to be in the present, enjoying nature.

Brief Grounding Exercises: Here are five short exercises that will help you experience and solidify each part of our grounding definition. I would recommend enjoying these grounding exercises often, perhaps doing them at least once a week.

Bring your spirit fully into your body,
suffusing the body with energy and light.

Put on a piece of your favorite inspiring music. Let the music flow into you, moving your body in any way it desires, to feel and express the joy of the music. Hold your hands out, palms open and receive the energy of spirit, allowing it to fill your heart. *Say the affirmation: "I have arrived."* to clarify your intention as spirit to fully embody your body.

Allow the physical and emotional body
to speak to you without repression.

Sit in a quiet place and scan your body for any place your attention is drawn to. Perhaps a part feels tight, sore, tired, or restless; perhaps a part feels particularly good. Begin to write in your journal whatever comes to mind as you focus on your body. Ask the part of your body that your attention is drawn to, "What is your message for me?" Just record your body's truth at this moment. When this feels complete, write about what you are feeling emotionally. Write "This is silly, I have nothing to say," if that is what comes. And just keep writing until you feel you have discovered how you feel at this moment. If you get stuck, write for a while with your non-dominant hand, the hand that you normally do not write with. This tends to bring out things that may be in your unconscious at the moment.

Feel your connection with the earth,
and allow its sacred energy into you.

If possible go to a beautiful place in nature that calls to you. From there or, even inside your home, give thanks to the earth for supporting your life, praise the wonderful things about being on earth for you, and send your love to the earth. Then open to allow the earth's energy and love to flow back into you. Receive the energy of each of the four elements: earth, air, fire, and water—imagining each as a color, sound, or smell.

Be fully spirit and flesh at the same time.

After completing the above earth exercise, continue as follows: Allow the earth energies to continue to flow into you through your feet or, if sitting, through the base of your spine. At the same time hold your hands up, palms open and bring in the highest energy of spirit, imagining this as a color, sound, or smell. Let all these earth and heaven energies meet in your heart, to blend and then suffuse throughout your body, allowing yourself to glow with light and be anchored with the strength of the earth at the same time.

Be fully in the present moment.

Sit quietly and watch your thoughts. If they flick to the past or the future, just gently bring them back to observing what is going to around you and inside you at this very moment. *Say the affirmation: "I am here."*

How does happiness relate to this manifestation essential we call grounding? As mentioned, grounding is chiefly driven by your intention to be fully here in the present moment. It stands to reason that unless you are very happy to be experiencing whatever is going on, part of your attention will be attempting to get away from it and your grounding will be less firm.

I want to mention that all the energies that we will be talking about in this book including gratitude, love, and happiness are often thought of as emotional responses to events that occur around us. For example, we feel grateful when something good happens to us, loving when someone loves us, and happy when things are going well for us. Looking at these energies in this manner diminishes them to reactions out of our control to the environment around us. And it implies that we need certain events or circumstances in order to experience these energies and if negative events are occurring, then our only options are to be ungrateful, unloving, and unhappy.

In order to have these important energies for manifestation available to us on a consistent basis we are going to be looking at them as states of consciousness that we can generate, increase, and sustain by applying proven strategies for bringing these positive energies forth regardless of the circumstances around us. We do have a choice whether we will experience these energies frequently or experience their opposites. This is a much more powerful and responsible position.

Are you happy to be here????

"Happy to be here" means happy to be in a physical body. This can be challenge if your body feels weak, sluggish, in pain, etc. So it becomes important to provide your body what it needs to be in joy including great nutrition, proper rest, exercise, and just allowing that body's joy in movement to be expressed. And it is important to the extent that you can to alleviate any pain and tension through medical care, massage, yoga, etc.

"Happy to be here" means happy to be on this particular planet at this time. This can be very challenging because of many things. We may have lost loved ones that we miss terribly. We may be overwhelmed with the amount of pain, stupidity, and greed we see in the world around us. We may feel a constant grinding pressure to support ourselves and to protect our loved ones. I personally suffered from significant depression from when I was about eight years old and continuing until my thirties. Many times there were days that started with the thought, "Should I slit my throat or get out of bed?" followed by an extreme act of will just to put one foot in front of the other and go on with the day. I kept these thoughts private because they felt shameful, given how much better off I knew I was compared to many people on planet Earth, and this shame isolated me further.

It is important here to come to whatever philosophical or spiritual stance we need to hold the polarities, both pleasant and unpleasant, of physical life with a sense of peace. I found in my life that many things about being here on this planet, such as my brother's suicide, just broke my heart. So I divorced myself from the common cultural image of a broken heart and developed a different image of my heart as a vast ocean. If you come into my life and my heart now, it is like a hand being put into water. There is no resistance and you are completely embraced. If you leave, the water goes back to complete, perhaps losing a drop. With this ocean heart image I can hold the pain of a loved one's struggles, the futility of war, etc., and maintain my sense of peace and being happy to be here on this beautiful planet. It does not mean that I no longer care or stop doing things to improve what I care about. But it does mean that I don't have to escape from the present and into activities that numb my mind and emotions. I help myself to stay in touch with the positive by avoiding broadcast news and being around negative people, and instead read stories about the good here; and I enjoy the planet's beauty whenever I can.

"Happy to be here" means happy to be in this relationship, this job, this community, this neighborhood, and this home. Unhappiness can be an insistent and persistent guidance that you need to change attitude, perspective, or circumstance. And finally "Happy to be here" means happy to be experiencing exactly what you are experiencing in this sacred moment.

Wow, that is a lot to happiness to keep track of! In the Liquid Luck meditation you are guided, just for the meditation time at least and hopefully longer, to be happy as you create a powerful abundance tool. The good news is that happiness is really not so much about having everything in all areas of life going the way you think they should and having every material thing that you can dream of. Rather it is an attitude about life, other people, and yourself that allows happiness and peace amidst whatever is going on in your life. Let's see how this can be accomplished and more about the power of happiness.

Of course we are not talking about a "stiff upper lip" kind of false happiness—that just won't cut it for powerfully creating your dreams. Rather we are aiming for a genuine joy of life, a real *joie de vive*—the French expression meaning a cheerful enjoyment of life; an exultation of spirit. *Joie de vivre* may be seen as a joy of everything, a comprehensive joy, a philosophy of life. Proponents of self-actualization such as Abraham Maslow or Carl Rogers saw happiness as one of the by-products of the rediscovery of what the latter called "the quiet joy in being one's self . . . a spontaneous relaxed enjoyment, a sense of play, and of access to the true self."

The even better news is that you don't have to be perfect in this for it to work very well. It is more of a continuum—if you are 90 percent happy in any or all areas of life, that is extremely powerful—the more areas the better. If you are now 50 percent happy you can indeed learn to cultivate happiness, and as you move toward a greater percent happy, you will notice immediate improvement in your manifestation power.

Happiness is so important that the right of everyone to pursue happiness is a sacred clause in the United States Declaration of Independence. Yet, I am fairly dismayed as a psychologist that so much of the profession's time has been wrapped up in understanding dysfunction and depression in its many forms. Fortunately there is a fairly new movement within psychology, called Positive Psychology which is beginning to look at happiness and thriving, and how these occur, sometimes even in very un-ideal circumstances. An excellent book on this is Martin Seligman's *Authentic Happiness*, written in 2002, which followed his bestseller, *Learned Optimism*.

One interesting study that Seligman mentions is a longitudinal study following nuns before their taking vows in 1932 throughout the next six decades of their lives. The advantage here is that all 178 nuns were experiencing essentially the same life-style, diet, social class, access to medical care, etc. Yet there was still much variation in health and longevity. Using their admissions essay written when they joined the order, the study found that of those nuns writing the most cheerful essays at that time, 90 percent were alive at eighty-five, versus only 34 percent of the least cheerful essay writers—and 54 percent were still alive at ninety-four, versus only 11 percent of the least happy as judged by that initial essay.

An even simpler indicator in another study concluded that women who had a genuine smile in their college graduation picture were more likely to experience personal well-being over the next thirty years, versus those who had an inauthentic smile. Scientists can tell the difference in smiles because different muscles are moved in a genuine smile. Psychologists also find that events and things can produce happiness but it is often fleeting. Their studies indicate that enduring happiness is based more on values and character strengths. Valuing behaviors such as forgiving and forgetting, and love and kindness encourages happiness. Cultivating strengths such as wisdom, curiosity, open-mindedness, integrity, and courage also tend to produce long-term happiness. I talked to a twenty-one million dollar lottery winner and she said that for three months she and her partner were on cloud nine, then things began to settle down and normalize. They love having the money and the things they can do with it for their family and causes. Yet most of the issues that were there before the windfall remain to be dealt with.

While it is very helpful to have major sources of stress such as conflict, joblessness, and disease under control, that tends to produce more of a sense of safety and peace. True joy is only loosely associated with material wealth. In fact there are many countries where people report being happier than those living in the USA, with much less income at their disposal.

A study[1] from 2011 found that participants who were ninety-five and older lived no more virtuous lives than the general population when it came to healthy behaviors (meaning smoking, eating, and exercises habits). As I write this chapter Dr. Alexander Imich at one hundred eleven years old has been crowned the world's oldest living man, according to Guinness World Records. His motto, is that one should "always pursue what one loves and is passionate about." I could not agree more.

So what do we glean from all this? While there may be a natural range of happiness that varies from person to person, one can learn to live at the top of one's happiness range by cultivating certain beliefs, attitudes, behaviors, and experiences—many of which we will be talking about in this book, as they also enhance abundance creation and luck. Long-term happiness is not likely to be achieved by the acquiring of things, rather it blossoms by achieving positive attitudes.

To shift beliefs that hamper happiness can be challenging. We are social creatures and live in a cultural context. When we look at western culture we see a very deep underpinning belief that happiness is suspect, that it is not genuine. Starting from the concept of original sin, it is suggested that we are intrinsically damaged and heaven is someplace else, which is strange in that even Christ was reported to have said that the kingdom of heaven is within. If religion portrays this planet as a veil of tears, it is then easy for other ideas to coalesce around this. Science concluded many years ago that the prime directive of nature is survival of the fittest (not the happiest). It is my opinion that Bruce Lipton in *The Biology of Belief* has

---

1 http://www.livescience.com/15362-live-100-longevity-good-genes.html

disproven this tenet and provides good evidence that nature's prime directive is actually "for the good of all."

This cultural pessimism is given voice in phrases such as "Waiting for the other shoe to fall,"; "Be careful what you want, you just might get it,"; "Nothing good comes easy,"; "No pain no gain"; and many more sayings that suggest that happiness is not our natural state and can be fleeting and dangerous. In fact the scientific study of the nuns, studies of who suffers from heart disease and survives, and many more studies show that happiness enhances our chances of a healthy, safe, and productive life. There is a field of medicine called psychoneuroimmunology that studies how hormones and health are affected by emotions. It too rates happiness as one of the best things one can experience to increase health. So go ahead! Try it—be happy! Move away from "No pain no gain" and "Nothing good comes easy," to a more open stance where you acknowledge the power and frequency of grace and blessings, and that it is okay for you to receive all good and to enjoy it thoroughly.

Develop empowering, joyful attitudes and behaviors that leave room for you to see the goodness in yourself and others, and to celebrate and express that goodness. Replace seeking an-eye-for-an-eye justice with fostering mercy and forgiveness. Allow yourself to be optimistic and don't feel foolish for doing so.

Let go easily. When I find myself tempted to righteous indignation, feeling victimized, and plotting revenge, I remember the saying, "Never attribute to malice what you can account for by stupidity!" It is very rare that someone is actually out to get you, hold you down, or prevent your success. Usually they are just not thinking of your needs and they are viewing the situation very differently. Opening communication with them can help with this, as most people would like to be helpful to you if they understand what you need and are treated in turn with respect.

It can be very helpful in moving away from the negativity and stress of our culture to surround yourself with optimistic, affirming, and happy people. There are several relatives and friends that I am blessed to know that just elevate my spirit every time I am with them. Take the time to be with these people whoever they are in your life. Seek them out as a real treasure and begin to fade your time spent with those who judge, criticize, compete, and proclaim endlessly about all that is wrong with the world.

Put less time and energy into acquiring things and make time and energy available for experiences that you know you enjoy, such as listening to great music, being out in nature, baking cookies from scratch, whatever absorbs your interests. Make a play list of songs that to you celebrate happiness and listen when you need a boost. Happy activities can be simple and inexpensive. It can be more satisfying to enjoy a good cup of coffee with a dear friend than to go on a whirlwind vacation, though that can be great fun too with the right attitude. Giving yourself freedom to play, to laugh, to be silly, to try new things and not be good at them, to change routine. Look up "Laughing Buddha on Subway" and "Divine Laughter" on YouTube and see the power of one person's laughter. There is a Buddhist proverb that, "Laughter is the language of the Gods."

One of the most important things you can do is simple (but at times not easy)—just decide to be happy. You can help yourself with this by starting and ending each day with a few moments of something that you really enjoy. Be happy about at least part of the situation you find yourself in at any given time. My brother John was challenged by a disease called Inclusion Body Myositis, which is similar to ALS, where all the voluntary muscles waste away. He had a feeding tube because he couldn't swallow and was on a ventilator much of the time to help with his breathing and was confined to a wheel chair. At the time I wrote the first draft of this chapter he only could speak quietly for short period with great effort. John lived next door to me. The disease is fatal and he died while I was writing this book. I loved going to see him even during the last weeks of his life because he said he still looked forward to the day. When there visiting with him, it was obvious that he was happy to see me, and celebrated the good fortune in other's lives and a myriad of other things.

Feeling happy makes it much easier for us to begin to think more positively. And thinking positively is a very powerful manifestation tool, as emphasized by Norman Vincent Peale in *The Power of Positive Thinking*, and by other many authors and empowerment leaders since. Positive thought tends to bring positive experiences to us in this free choice universe that resonates with what we are thinking and feeling, feeding it back to us in events, people, and experiences. For proof just smile genuinely at a few people you meet during the day and most likely most of them will smile back at you. Or joyfully help someone each day and experience the increase in people "spontaneously" offering to help you.

I think that we would be happier if we treated ourselves like a dog, meaning a favorite pet. When I think of how we treat a beloved pet dog, I am reminded that we thrive best when we extend similar kindnesses toward ourselves. I would never say to my pet that it is fat, old, or ugly, yet I might still criticize myself for my perceived imperfections. Given that DNA in a test tube responds to positive emotions and language, it stands to reason that so do we, so it is important to praise and talk positively and lovingly to yourself. We all need to hear "*good dog*" many times a day!

I always make sure to take my dog for daily walks outside, rain or shine. My spirit enjoys being out as well so that I can take in beauty of nature. When I see how happily my dog reacts to seeing old friends, I am reminded to give my friends a call and make time to see them, even if it involves flying across the country once in a while to do so. My dog shows pleasure so openly at being hugged and petted, it reminds me to hug, and schedule that massage long delayed because of an overly full calendar. My dog enjoys her routines but absolutely loves going somewhere new and makes no effort to contain her excitement and explorations while there. We respond well to new places and experiences as well, so schedule that vacation to a new location—even if it's a daytrip to explore a neighborhood or park you've never been to in your area.

Finally, my dog is not afraid of stopping and resting when tired, content to be around loved ones and stare into space, relaxing, then gradually and naturally falling asleep with no concern for the clock. We benefit from the gift of quiet relaxation time as well, so we can be ready for the next call to action whether it be dinner, a walk, a new toy to play with, or person to meet.

In case you were wondering, I love cats too. Mine inspires me mainly to be relaxed and graceful, to do my own thing, to ask for what I want, and to not fret about what anyone else thinks!

When you treat yourself as well as you treat your beloved pet, you honor yourself as a most important guest at the feast table of your own life. And the universe in turn, responds by treating you as such, with great manifestations of abundance and good fortune. I often use this affirmation: "I welcome myself as most honored guest in my own heart." For me it counters old tendencies to put myself last and deny myself satisfaction by focusing too much on struggle and work.

Another powerful way to generate happiness is to allow ourselves to feel grateful. We will explore the powerful energy of gratitude in the next chapter. It is the next energy after happiness that as a wizard of great wisdom and power, you put into your Liquid Luck energy elixir.

Chapter 2

GRATITUDE

Just another exciting moment from my Liquid Luck Listening. I am almost 70, and for all those years I have been looking for a four-leaf clover, that most lucky of symbols. I have lived on two continents and in three countries and always watched out for a four-leaf clover, never ever found one in all these years. This morning I was walking my dog when I looked down and there at my feet, sitting slightly apart from the other clover plants, was a four-leaf clover looking right at me. My mother used to sing that song to us all the time, "I'm looking over a four-leaf clover that I overlooked before" and I could hear her singing as I knelt down and carefully, apologetically, picked the precious little thing. I am putting it inside a book to dry properly. Imagine! Seventy years, and I finally found one! It's gotta be Liquid Luck! —V.A.

From the Liquid Luck Meditation: *Then say "I am Grateful"... feel gratitude and send gratitude, concentrating it into your elixir, thinking of all the wonderful blessings in your life and feeling your gratitude for them, and sending this energy into your potion.*

In the Liquid Luck meditation, after allowing happiness to flower, one is next guided to feel gratitude which is the feeling and expression of appreciation for what one has or experiences. Feelings of thankfulness and appreciation open up one's heart energy even further, and increase awareness of the good we are already receiving. This helps us to be open and ready for more blessings to flow to us. One of my fellow trainers at The Monroe Institute and a good friend, Franceen King, is fond of putting it this way, "The attitude of gratitude creates the space for grace." This concept is also compatible with the principle of "Like attracts like," espoused in Ester and Jerry Hicks *The Law of Attraction*, recently popularized by the movie *The Secret*. Deeply and consistently feeling happiness, gratitude, and other positive emotions tends to bring us positive experiences.

True gratitude is very joyful (happiness again). It is very different from the feelings generated when someone tells us, "You should be grateful receiving a gift (that you didn't want and looks useless to you) for your birthday. Now write that thank you note this minute!" That is not gratitude, rather that is a feeling of duty or obligation to be grateful when you are not feeling grateful at all.

Melody Beattie, in *Gratitude: Inspirations*, says, "Gratitude unlocks the fullness of life. It turns what we have into enough, and more. It turns denial into acceptance, chaos to order, confusion to clarity. It can turn a meal into a feast, a house into a home, a stranger into a friend."

Melanie Greenberg, psychologist, in *The Mindful Self* states: "Experiencing and expressing gratitude is an important part of any spiritual practice. It opens the heart and activates positive emotion centers in the brain. Regular practice of gratitude can change the way our brain neurons fire into more positive automatic patterns. The positive emotions we evoke can soothe distress and broaden our thinking patterns so we develop a larger and more expansive view of our lives.

Gratitude is an emotion of connectedness, which reminds us we are part of a larger universe with all living things."

Gratitude is associated in psychology studies with increased levels of energy, optimism, and empathy. It can be cultivated. One way is to take a moment each day to express appreciation to someone who has been helpful to you. Thank someone for good service as you leave a tip, or email a company expressing appreciation for their product. Say to yourself or express to another that you are grateful for the sunrise, or discovering a delicious new recipe—it can be anything and it does not need to be something big. If someone thanks you rather than answering with, "Oh it was nothing," say that it was your pleasure and tell them why.

I would like you to imagine a miracle planet with me. Imagine that this planet has a symphony orchestra with over fifty trillion members which can play an incredible variety of music and play each piece perfectly. Within this grand symphony there are many sub-orchestras each playing something different but somehow harmonious with whatever grand song is playing at the moment. All this goes on seamlessly even though billions of new members join or leave the symphony's ranks each day.

Now imagine that the symphony has simultaneously five conductors who are only partially aware of each other and yet manage to conduct in a way that allows beautiful songs to flow. And additionally, that each of the conductors can call at a second's notice for a change in song and the orchestra will instantly and seamless shift to the new song required. Furthermore this symphony can play around the clock without even a second's break for more than a hundred years without stopping.

Such a symphony has to be judged as such an impossibility that it could only be called a miracle. Yet on this wondrous planet there are billions of such symphonies, 99 percent of which coexist cooperatively and peacefully.

Yes, this miracle planet and miracle symphony we are imagining does exist. The symphony is your body. The conductor you are most aware of is your conscious mind which is often barely aware of the other conductors which are the intelligence centers in your unconscious mind, your heart, your gut, and your spirit. The fifty trillion orchestra members, replaced by the billions daily are the cells of your body. The songbook the orchestra plays is life, and indeed you can change the song at a moment's notice from calm and serene, even asleep, to awake and engaging in a nearly infinite variety of moods or activities.

In fact the whole symphony started with just one member, the one-celled zygote from the Greek word for joined, formed from the union of egg and sperm. And this one cell then seamlessly maintained the song of life through division into the fifty trillion members of the adult human body, handling amazing changes along the way. This is the miracle and power of the human genetic code. The complexity of your body symphony is so staggering that it is hard to begin to grasp and sometimes it is easier just to contemplate a small part of it such as the beauty and the complexity of the song of the human hand.

Watching the Olympics, or a Cirque du Soleil show can give you an idea of the body's capacity for inspiring endurance and beautiful movement. It saddened me as a psychotherapist to meet many people who felt that their body was something to be ashamed of and gross. It saddens me when I see so many people believing the "news" that we are horrible creatures who are constantly at war and trying to scam one another. If there are six million people at war today, that means that there more than seven billion people at peace today, so less than a tenth of one percent are at war. This is the real news—that we are peaceful creatures with very, very few exceptions.

Why bring up the miracle of the human body in a chapter about gratitude? My reason is three-fold: First, you need look no further than your own body to be filled with gratitude, awe, and appreciation for its sacredness and its gift to you of life. And sending gratitude to your body is an extremely powerful action. I believe doing so will enliven your body, improve your health, allow much greater energy to flow for manifestation, and open the great wisdom channel of the body from which you can receive invaluable guidance.

Second, contemplating the miracle of your body can lead you to see that we are constantly surrounded by miracles of every ilk and variety all of the time, and much like awareness of the air we breathe we often lose awareness of just how special this is. When we experience always living within miracle space, then the miracle of healing, or manifesting what we desire to create are seen as a more seamless part of our nature, and not highly unlikely outlying events that only the exceptional can enjoy on a very rare basis.

And third, having great gratitude for your body and the life it supports helps you with the grounding (being fully in the present moment and fully in touch with your body) mentioned in the previous chapter on happiness, which we have seen is highly important to manifestation power.

Gratitude is a powerful attractant for people to want to help you, even without being asked. Other people are often essential in manifesting what we desire and supporting us in enjoying what we have. Think of a person in your life for whom you have done much, but who seldom if ever expresses thanks back to you. Even if you love them, their lack of gratitude can make you feel like pulling away because the energy exchange is unequal and leaves you feeling drained and perhaps even resentful. You might even have a service job where you are constantly extending yourself for others and they seldom express appreciation back. Maybe they think why should they bother expressing thanks as you are been paid to serve them. Or maybe it is in your role as parent, child, or spouse that others think you are just doing what is expected and should not be thanked. If you want to manifest powerfully in your life and have all the support that the universe wants to give you through other people, you do not want to be this ungrateful person. If fact you want to shine true and genuine gratitude to all you meet for them being in your life and helping you along your path.

An exercise that you can use to practice gratitude is to write a letter once a week to some organization that you feel is doing good work and/or has personally benefited you. I feel that these letters often reach just the right person on the right day to make them feel better about how they are spending their lives. Here is an example of such a letter that I wrote recently. It does not need to be fancy to be appreciated.

Maybins Garbage Service

Dear Maybins Company,

I want to write a thank-you note to you for the excellent service provided by your company to us for the last many years. You have come once per week very reliably. Your drivers are cheerful and leave the site clean at all times. When we have called your company, your staff has been courteous, helpful, and professional every time we have interacted with them. You prices have remained reasonable as the years have passed.

For your service quality to be this excellent we know that everyone at your company must work together well, be highly professional, and take pride in their roles at the company—including the owners, office staff, drivers, and mechanics.

In these stressful days in is wonderful to have something go so well and pleasantly on such a regular basis that you can relax and trust that they will continue to exceed expectations. It even feels like your are part of our extended family!

Very best wishes,

Joe and Elena Gallenberger

Just as I was putting these thoughts to print I received an email from one of my students. In it she stated:

Hi Joe—just wanted to share that in my experience, manifestation proceeds almost effortlessly once one

embraces gratitude practice. I mean being grateful for EVERYTHING that enters one's life, recognizing that each event has a sacred purpose, even the unpleasant ones. Sending lots of love to you and Elena.
—*M. W.*

I would like to close this chapter by discussing how gratitude and happiness relate to one another. Often we view it as "I feel grateful because I am happy with something." One can also look at it the other way around: "When I am grateful, I am happy." Gratitude can be a powerful generator of happiness. Here gratefulness involves becoming aware of something that we have been given without effort or money on our part. In fact each present moment is given to us each day. And each moment presents us with the opportunity to either enjoy the present moment or the opportunity to change attitudes or circumstance so that we can enjoy the next present moment more fully. If we are aware of the continuous gift of present moments given to us freely, and the miracle of our human body symphony, we can live from a place of consistent gratitude and therefore be happy almost all of the time.

Chapter 3

ABUNDANCE

Hi you guys. Well, I will throw my story in too for the Liquid Luck collection. I got a real surprise this morning. It's the end of the month and I usually budget carefully at this time of month just before pension day. Getting ready to take the dog out for his walk, I selected a pair of socks I seldom wear from my sock drawer. I don't know when I last wore those socks. As I went to put them on, something crinkled in the toe of one. Surprised, I reached in and out tumbled five twenty dollar bills. I must have hidden them on myself almost a year ago. It's been a while since I wore those socks. My dog got a nice treat at the store!! I had just listened to the Liquid Luck CD for the second time last night before I went to bed. There is nothing like the sight of fresh green cash when you don't expect it. —V.R.

From the Liquid Luck Meditation: *Next say "I am abundant" . . . feel abundant, and send the energy of abundance, remembering all the ways in which you are already highly abundant and sending this energy into your liquid.*

Dictionary definitions of abundance include terms such as overflowing fullness, abundance of the heart, and an ample supply. Here we are referring to the broad idea of true wealth in all areas of life including health, nurturing relationships, meaningful career, supportive community, and also a flow of money sufficient not only for basic needs but to fully express one's self in work and play and to help others. We do not mean just a narrow focus on how much money or possessions we may have. We are referring to a feeling which only loosely correlates to the particular quantity of money we have. It is obvious that many who are rich may not enjoy any feeling of abundance and many who have less countable assets may feel grandly rich. So abundance is partly a measure of our skill at perceiving the wealth we already do have, from the basic gift of this day to live, through the free gifts of the beauty of nature, a body, access to cultural experiences, love, and other things that cost not a penny.

Feeling abundant should be easier to accomplish than it is. The difficulty comes in part from what many have called our chattering monkey mind which persists in comparing ourselves constantly with others. And this ego-mind tends to ignore those who appear to have less and weigh more heavily any indication that others may have more. If fact it can even single out one aspect such as financial wealth or a fancier car and ignore that we may have more friends, health, joy, or freedom from debt than the person with the fancy car. It almost seems that our monkey mind is invested in keeping us from feeling abundant and therefore happy.

Ego-mind may be there to keep us from feeling complacent and to measure our status compared to others in our tribe. Therefore at its most basic it is probably trying to keep us safe. But it often does so at the expense of us feeling happy, content, and complete. And our individual ego-mind has a lot of help from the current cultural mind-set in most "developed" nations. The culture has a strong investment in fueling our feeling of the opposite of abundance, and instead feeling scarcity and lack. In fact capitalism and control require this. Yes, a regulated capitalism designed to ensure fairness and balance can be a tremendously vibrant system which nurtures innovation, risk, and change, and rewards intelligence and hard work. And it is a better system in practice than any other we have come up with so far, such as communism. So how did this empowering system of capitalism get off track?

It is important to understand this for meaningful discussion of abundance so while mentioned in *Inner Vegas: Creating Miracles Abundance and Health*, I want to expand on it here.

From my point of view the physical and non-physical universes are both abundant beyond measure. Some examples are:

Physical numbers—Witness the countless numbers of species of plants and animals and the huge numbers in many species' individual populations, such as the number of trees on the earth. And the latest estimates from telescopes is that there are 400 billion galaxies each containing billions of stars. Just eighty years ago we thought there was just one galaxy.

Energy—The sun, oceans, and wind contain energy in uncountable measure. Science has begun exploring zero-point energy that exists in incomprehensible quantity even in the near vacuum of outer space.

Love—Each of us has the opportunity to love each of the other billions of humans on earth, plus many animals that can respond to our love.

Beauty—We are free to enjoy music, warmth, rain, and sun, sunsets, mountains, and oceans. If we open our perception we can see beauty nearly everywhere from the smallest leaf to the grandest mountain range.

Humor—If we have a sense of humor, particularly about ourselves, opportunities for laughter abound.

With this grand abundance around us and many more kinds that have not been mentioned, how can we possibly be plagued with feelings of scarcity and lack? We have mentioned ego-mind's tricks that are probably trying to keep us safe. But this tendency is greatly encouraged by the general culture's continual creation of messages and stories that provoke ego-mind into overdrive by suggesting that we are lacking in something important.

Why would various cultural institutions create such messages? I feel that it is because promoting feelings of lack allows those in power to sell us something. Those in power, be they religious, scientific, educational, economic, or political want us to believe that it is dangerous, hostile, and scarce out there. And only they have the one true way out of lack, and into control, pleasure, and peace. If we believe them, then we will comply with their demands in order to be safe and happy.

Religion says that we are sinful creatures unable to contact the Divine directly by ourselves, who need to be guided to salvation or we will burn in some type of hell . And tithing to them will help us stay on the path. Institutional science says that religion is wrong, that there is no god and that if we don't rely on what we can prove by its methods, we will burn each other at the stake of superstition. Science proclaims objectivity but in fact is influenced heavily by political and philosophical bias, and economic forces, often becoming a type of religion unto itself. The educational system requires that school be compulsory, asserting that without such formal training we will be ignorant, unskilled, and unable to compete for scarce resources. Yet the system often stifles creativity and ingenuity, and is also heavily politicized. The political system says we lack the ability to get along and be fair with each other and that without its leadership we would be in chaos and ruin. The governments around the world proclaims that they protect our freedom and safety but have in many places become the chief threat to both freedom and safety.

Capitalism require consumers, so advertising bombards us with messages about what we lack and provokes ego-mind to feel restless and at times even desperate unless we have the "best" of everything. It even encourages us to go into debt to purchase what promises to make us happy.

We want to fit in, be good people, do right, and to be successful, so it's difficult not to listen to these messages coming at us from so many directions, and we usually end up with feeling of lack (a truly abundance-killing way to feel) and a life-pattern of struggle. We struggle to have enough money, take enough vitamins, get enough exercise, have enough of the right kind of friends, live in the right neighborhood, and then we are surprised when we find ourselves tired, and say that we don't have enough time or energy to keep up!

This is not resonant with who we truly are! We can instead choose to be aware of the reality of abundance and empower ourselves to feel abundant in everyday life regardless of almost any circumstance.

As mentioned, abundance refers both to an objective ample amount of something such as health or finances, but it is also a feeling of what we have being ample and a feeling of gratitude for it. The good news is that our feelings of abundance are highly under our control by what we choose to focus upon. We can be strong and wise enough to ignore institutional ploys suggesting scarcity and compassionately quiet our ego-mind by moving into our heart's wisdom and appreciating all the grand flow of abundance we do have on a moment to moment basis simply by the fact of being alive.

Feeling abundance strongly and consistently tends to create more objective abundance. Given the feeling of prosperity is so subjective, the ground is fertile and ready for transforming any feeling of lack into a humble celebration of our own personal abundance, and strong connection with the abundance of the world around us. After a personal crisis such as a house fire or a heart attack, often people report a dramatic resetting of their feelings about what is important, and a celebration of the nonmaterial things as being of highest value such as family, health, friends, and life itself.

A great way to reset and enhance our feeling of abundance without the need for an unpleasant personal crisis is to use affirmations regularly. Affirmations are short visualizations or statements of how you will look at reality and yourself. They are most effective in positive language and present tense. They are designed to be written, spoken, or sung. They are repeated until they penetrate and affect your consciousness. Affirmations are a wonderful way to counteract the hypnosis of lack that the culture continually sends forth. You can also use affirmations to find resistance. For example, the affirmation, "*I deserve great wealth*" may result in the reaction: "Who me? I am not that special." This can point to issues of undeservingness that need to be cleared for abundance to come to you. Such issues of self-imposed restriction can be easily picked up as a child if our needs are not met.

Affirmations can clear your thinking and focus your intent. Please review these sample abundance affirmations and use any that feel particularly useful to you. It is also helpful to create some of your own, as your own words and images can be very powerful for you.

- I am free of all limits.

- I am of great light.

- I am of great love.

- I feel full joy at the beauty of the human spirit.

- I receive my energy to overflowing from unlimited and always available Source.

- Money is a manifestation of the light I fully open to now.

- My receiving enables freedom on all levels.

- I invite prosperity for the sheer pleasure of it.

- I now enjoy life to the fullest.

- I am abundant in all matters of the physical.

- All is abundance.

- I give myself everything that I would my beloved.

It can be fun and powerful to put your affirmation intent into a simple song and sing it to yourself. This is an example of a song, sung to the tune of *Row, Row, Row, Your Boat* that friends shared with me and gave me permission to share with you. Please give it a try by singing it out loud—it is just about guaranteed to make you feel good!

Money is only energy
(Row, Row, Row, Your Boat),
that comes easily to me
(gently down the stream)
I love money and money loves me
(Merrily, merrily, merrily, merrily)
and I create it easily!
(Life is but a dream).

Affirmations can also take the form of prayer. There is much wonderful spiritual thought in this world. Please permit me to offer an example from the Christian tradition, The Lord's Prayer. This prayer was Jesus' response to the question, "How should we pray?" The traditional Greek-based translation is as follows:

"Our Father who art in heaven hallowed be thy Name.
Thy kingdom come, thy will be done, on earth as it is in
heaven. Give us this day our daily bread and forgive us
our trespasses as we forgive those who trespass against us.
Lead us not into temptation, but deliver us from evil.
For thine is the kingdom, the power and glory forever
and ever. Amen."

Notice that the usual Greek contains a series of petitions. *"Give us this day . . . Forgive us our trespasses . . . Deliver us from evil."*

Jesus himself spoke Aramaic, which is a highly contextual language. It has been proposed that a more accurate translation of the original Aramaic contains affirmations instead of petitions. And this confirms our abundance. It is as follows:

> *"Our Father, who is everywhere in the universe, your name is sacred. Your kingdom is among us; your will is throughout the earth as it is throughout the universe. You give us our needful bread from day to day and you forgive us our offenses even as we forgive our offenders. You do not let us enter into materialism, but you separate us from error. For yours is the kingdom, and the power, and the song, from ages to ages, sealed in faithfulness.*

When I guide people into meditations to visualize what they would like to create in their lives, I recommend that as they relax at the beginning of the meditation, they call to mind some way in which they are already abundant. This way, all feeling of lack vanishes and what they would like to manifest next becomes the cherry on top of the already wonderful sundae that is their life.

As I am writing this chapter, I have just written, voiced, and produced a new CD and download. My intuition has been guiding me to complete this project for four years. It is called *Abundance Waterfall: A meditation enhancing abundance flow in all areas of life*. In the meditation gentle words, binaural beats, and subtle nature sounds encourage you to relax, open your heart, and experience your very own Abundance Waterfall. You are guided to imagine a waterfall celebrating your current flow of abundance, and then to increase the flow in any and all areas of your life where you desire greater abundance—such as health, money, relationships, career, and spiritual life. You can of course use this imagery without the CD to increase your feelings of abundance.

Most manifestation exercises help you visualize one specific thing that you would like to manifest. Abundance Waterfall imagery enhances your awareness of the entire flow of abundance available to you and dramatically increases your capacity to receive it. This opens you to a flow of miracle blessings beyond your current experience. Early reports include:

"As a result of the powerful sonic impressions contained within Abundance Waterfall I experienced intense and extremely positive 3-D manifestation imagery in my mind."

"This is a unique way to approach abundance from the heart. Each time I have listened I have been filled with joy and light"

"I went to a delightful new place in consciousness that I had not been to before."

I took the time to produce Abundance Waterfall in the hope that it will benefit many people, because I know that cultivating consistent feelings of abundance is one of the most powerful things we can do to help us manifest more positively in our own lives. And given that feeling abundant reduces fear, if many of us feel more abundant together, it will help us manifest a more positive future for our communities and the world.

I would like to close this chapter by offering the following exercise to activate your feelings of abundance and gratitude. It will take some time to do this exercise but doing so can trigger a profound sense of the reality of your current abundance and open you up for an even greater flow.

Carve out a morning, afternoon or evening for yourself. Sit down in a comfortable place with a dozen sheets of paper and pencil, or use your computer if you like. After a few deep relaxing breaths start listing all the ways in which you have been and still are abundant in your life.

- List the abundance of pet animals that you have enjoyed. Remember the good times, pleasure and comfort they have provided and thank each for gracing your life.

- List the abundance of family members, remembering how they have helped, taught, comforted, and supported you, and thank them.

- List the abundance of friends that you have had in your life. Remember the laughter, and feelings of belonging, togetherness, and sharing, and thank each of them.

- List the abundance of teachers, coaches, and mentors you have had in your life. Note how they each have contributed to your experience and thank them.

- List the abundance of beautiful music that you have enjoyed, particularly pieces that help you be inspired, happy, or consoled and thank the composers and artists for their efforts.

- List the abundance of books in your life that have spoken to your soul, offered confirmation of your truth, entertained, and instructed you and thank the authors and publishers of these books.

- List the abundance of beauty that you have experienced, places in nature, artwork, architecture, etc., and thank them for gracing your life.

- Note the abundance of adventures that you have had and how much learning and enjoyment they have provided and thank them for being part of your life experience.

- List all the good foods that you have enjoyed, thinking of your favorites and thanking them, for the pleasure and sustenance that they have provided.

- List the activities in your life that give you pleasure, such as massage, playing games, sexual expression, sports, recreation activities, hobbies, and give thanks for experiencing them.

- List the spiritual experiences that you have had, those peak moments that have helped elevate and inspire you and thank them for being part of your life experience.

- List any other areas of abundance that come to you and celebrate and thank them as well.

If you have worked on a computer, print these lists. Read what you have written once again and then spread your abundance papers out—experiencing the overview and celebrating all the great wealth of experiences that you have enjoyed so far, and affirm that you are open to the abundance to come. I hope that this exercise is a very powerful experience for you.

WE HAVE BEEN FOCUSING on happiness, gratitude, and abundance and seeing how they relate to one another. We have seen how happiness is a choice which can improve our health and energy, how cultivating gratitude increases happiness and tempts others to help us toward our dreams, and how feeling abundant brings more abundance. These are indeed important energies for helping us create our reality according to our best dreams. Now we will begin to explore energies that will expand our awareness beyond ourselves and balance any tendency for what we have focused upon so far to be just about us.

Always be happy at others' good fortune. Doing so is a great barometer that your own attitudes are in the right place. There is a saying attributed to James Brilliant, "Please spare me the ghastly details of your own happiness." I find this saying quite funny, because there is truth to it. When someone goes on and on about how happy or abundant they are, it can be tempting to feel resentment or envy, particularly if at the time things are not going so well for us.

This reaction speaks to us having an underlying fear that there is not enough to go around and somehow their good fortune might restrict our access to similar blessings. When I feel this way I refer to it as my "missing the train" feeling, meaning it feels at that moment like everyone else is on the party train laughing and celebrating and I somehow am stuck at the station. I used to feel shame at such an ungracious thought. Now when I become aware of it, I see it as funny given what I know about abundance creation. When I feel this way, I remind myself that there is always another train and shift toward finding or creating the next opportunity. When I stay in my old "missed the train" pattern, the feelings are often followed by a loss in my life. When I move into the new pattern of thinking often I am rewarded by another train a' coming, sometimes within minutes, particularly in casinos where feedback is so quick.

Celebrate with anyone sharing how they are successful and happy, for it is indeed an abundant universe and you can use their story as an inspiration. Ask them how they accomplished their achievement. You might learn something that you can apply to your own situation.

Chapter 4

COMPASSION

Thank you so much for Liquid Luck! After listening, my credit card company noticed that several small fraudulent charges had been made on my card from 2011-2012 and they gave me a credit for the entire amount of $250! I can't wait to see what happens next. Here's what happened next: Income from my previously stagnant and very small business doubled in 2 weeks and is increasing daily! —D.R.

From the Liquid Luck Meditation: *Now say "I am compassionate" . . . Feel your beauty, dignity, and sacredness, and your compassionate connection with all beings in their beauty—and send this energy of compassion into your potion.*

Compassion is defined as sympathetic awareness of others' distress together with a desire to help. It is the feeling of empathy for others (resonating with or understanding what they are experiencing) combined with a desire to alleviate their suffering. Compassion has an emotional component, yet it is also rational because it is consistent with concepts such as fairness, justice, and the interdependence and unity of all life. It is consistent with ideas such as the Golden Rule, "Do onto others as you would have them do unto you"; and, "Whatever you do to the least of my brethren, you do to me." Compassion is the logical stance toward other beings both human and non-human, if one believes, along with state-of-the-art biological data on genetic sharing among organisms, that nature's prime directive is, "For the good of all" and not the distortion of Darwinian precepts, "Survival of the fittest." The etymology of "compassion" is Latin, meaning "co-suffering." implying that an aware person cannot be fully happy if that happiness is at the expense of others. Another derivation suggests compassion means *"to love together with."* It is considered a great virtue in most philosophies and religions.

The following information is distilled from *The Greater Good: The Science of a Meaningful Life*.[2] Scientists have started to map the biological basis of compassion and feel it may have an important evolutionary purpose. This research has shown that when we feel compassion, our heart rate slows down, we secrete the bonding hormone, oxytocin, and regions of the brain linked to empathy, care giving, and pleasure are activated. Preliminary findings suggest, moreover, that being compassionate can improve health, well-being, and relationships. And they're finding that compassion can be increased through targeted exercises and practice. Here are some of the most salient findings from this research so far.

- Compassion makes us feel good: Compassionate action (for example, giving to charity) activates pleasure circuits in the brain, and even very brief compassion training programs strengthen brain circuits for pleasure and reward and lead to lasting increases in self-reported happiness.

2 Greater Good, University of California Berkeley: http://greatergood. berkeley.edu/topic/compassion/definition

- Tuning in to other people in a kind and loving manner can reduce the risk of heart disease.

- Compassion training programs can make people more resilient to stress by lowering stress hormones and strengthening the immune response.

- Brain scans during loving-kindness meditations, suggest that, on average, compassionate people's minds focus less on what has gone wrong in their lives, or might go wrong in the future, and as a result, they're happier.

- Compassion helps make caring parents: Brain scans show that when people experience compassion, neural systems activate that are known to support parental nurturance and other care giving behaviors.

- Compassion helps make better spouses: Compassionate people are more optimistic and supportive when communicating with others.

- Compassion helps make better friends: Studies of college friendships show that when one friend sets the goal to support the other compassionately, both friends experience greater satisfaction and growth in the relationship.

- Restraining feelings of compassion erodes our commitment to moral principles.

- Employees who receive more compassion in their workplace see themselves, their co-workers, and their organization in a more positive light, report feeling more positive emotions such as joy and contentment, and are more committed to their jobs.

- The more compassionate societies—those that take care of their most vulnerable members, assist other nations in need, and have children who perform more acts of kindness—are the happier ones.

- Compassionate people are more socially adept, making them less vulnerable to loneliness, and loneliness has been shown to harm the immune system.

- Compassion links us together with our fellow men and women and all life. In manifestation work it is an excellent antidote for greed, fear, or any lack of balance. It is a chief caller of wisdom into our lives and is both a stimulus to, and a result of, an open heart.

Also from the *Greater Good* website we can see how to cultivate more compassion. Research suggests that compassion appears to be at least partially a result of our upbringing, culture, and life experiences. and it can be strengthened through practice. Compassion training programs are revealing how we can boost feelings of compassion in ourselves and others. Here are some excellent tips that emerged out of those programs, as well as other research.

- Look for commonalities: Seeing yourself as similar to others increases feelings of compassion. A recent study shows that something as simple as tapping your fingers to the same rhythm with a stranger increases compassionate behavior.

- Be calm and centered: When we let our mind become fearful in response to someone else's pain, we inhibit the biological systems that enable compassion.

- Encourage cooperation, not competition, even through subtle cues: A study showed that describing a game as a "Community Game" led players to cooperate and share a reward evenly; describing the same game as a "Wall Street Game" made the players more cutthroat and less honest.

- See people as individuals not abstractions. When presented with an appeal from an anti-hunger charity, people were more likely to give money after reading about a starving girl than after reading statistics on starvation—even when those statistics were combined with the girl's story.

- Don't blame others for their misfortune, when we do this we feel less concern for them.

- Understand that we are capable of making a difference even if just by praying for or sending good energy to the person. If we feel powerless we tend to curb our compassion.

- Notice and savor how good it feels to be compassionate.

- Research suggests compassion is contagious, so if you want to help compassion spread, lead by example and start by modeling kindness, particularly to children.

- Curb the ego's tendency to see yourself as superior to others. Research suggests that as people feel a greater sense of status over others, they feel less compassion.

- Hold your own energetic space. When we completely take on other people's suffering as our own, we risk feeling personally distressed, threatened, and overwhelmed. In some cases, this can even lead to burnout, apathy, or callousness. Instead, be receptive to understanding other people's feelings without adopting those feelings as your own.

Just as we have found that gratitude enhances happiness and that happiness is a key to positive manifestation, so too compassion is related directly to happiness and therefore becomes very important to powerful and positive manifestation. The Dalai Lama states: "If you want others to be happy, practice compassion. If you want to be happy yourself, practice compassion."

A Guide to Cultivating Compassion in Your Life, With 7 Practices by Leo Babauta[3] also offers much good advice, summarized here.

Babauta believes compassion to be one of the few things we can practice that will bring immediate and long-term happiness into our lives. He is not talking about short-term gratification but something that will bring true and lasting happiness. He feels that the key to developing compassion is to make it a daily practice.

---

3 A guide to Cultivating Compassion in Your life with 7 Practices by Leo Babauta: http://zenhabits.net/a-guide-to-cultivating-compassion-in-your-life-with-7-practices/

Babuata also notes scientific studies that suggest there are physical benefits to practicing compassion—people who practice it produce one hundred percent more DHEA, which is a hormone that counteracts the aging process, and 23 percent less cortisol—the "stress hormone." His guide contains seven different practices that you can try and perhaps incorporate into your everyday life. I have modified a few of my favorites here:

- We all need food and shelter and want love and respect. Acknowledge what you have in common with others, even folks who might seem weird or evil to you. This can boil down to, "Just like me, this person is seeking happiness in his/her life."

- Act daily to help ease the suffering of others, even in a small way. Offer a smile, or a kind word, or do an errand or chore for them, or just be willing to listen with your full attention as another person shares a problem that they are having. I have a friend who is a great manifester. As an entrepreneur with many companies, he is in airports often. Most people find that airports drag their energy down with all the rush and stress. He keeps his energy high by looking for those he can help on his way through the airport (with luggage, directions, etc.). I tried this, and it works very well in just about any public situation that can be stressful such as malls and government buildings.

- An advanced stage of compassion is to not only to act to ease the suffering of those we love and give to charities that we resonate with, but to also act kindly even to those who mistreat us. Ideally, we can make each person we interact with into either a friend or into a teacher of how to stand our ground in a compassionate way. Imagine what stresses the person might be under. Practice acting with compassion the next time a person treats you poorly. You can start small. Practice allows this to feel more natural and shows you that it can be very rewarding.

For many people I think that the most challenging step is to practice self-compassion. To this end I often use the affirmation, "I accept myself as my most honored guest in my own heart" with great results. It seems to calm me down and open me up to all the good that the universe would like to send me. Really see your own beauty. You have probably had the experience of holding a newborn baby and your heart melting perhaps even to tears with love for the child. You know that you are becoming self-compassionate when you can think of yourself and feel as much love for yourself as you have felt toward that child in your arms. Lord knows that you have had your individual challenges and probably have encountered many things that broke your heart or weighed you down. You deserve the deepest of compassion as all feeling creatures do for being alive on a very tough planet and having to live with the consequences, however dire, of all your decisions, even those made with incomplete or distorted information.

My model of abundance is to fill yourself to overflowing with goodness of all types including self-compassion, and then share your overflow with others freely and compassionately. This is quite different than feeling sorry for someone. Pity puts you above them and disrespects the dignity, sacredness, and mystery of their journey. Attempts to help someone while feeling pity for them tends to result in efforts to help them your way, which can result in resistance in them and burnout in you.

As this book progresses I hope that you can see that the high energies discussed greatly empower our ability to manifest and heal. Conversely, if you use a technique such as Liquid Luck and then countermand it by living in greed, fear, ego, and "survival of the fittest" mentality and emotions, then life becomes like a battlefield and it is likely that not much good will result. This is in line with quantum physics and "Like Attracts Like" ideas that we are in a free choice reality and what we choose to think and feel most regularly will be reflected in our reality. It simply does not work to be wanting health, financial abundance, and great relationships, and then living deep within fear and struggle. It can be said that such miracle manifestations as we are talking about are impossible until they are easy. This is because struggle and effort really do not work in terms of manifesting the highest and best. Rather as we move into the high energies of happiness, gratitude, feeling abundant, and compassionate, then beautiful manifestations begin to flower, appearing almost to arise on their own. As we shall see as we move forward, there are still a few more energies that greatly enhance our ability as abundance creators.

Chapter 5

LOVE

On the morning after listening for the second time my dogs accidentally escaped through my front door that was open and I "just happened" to be looking out my bedroom window when they ran through the backyard, and I went downstairs and got them back in. Then I went to work, where I knew I was getting laid off and another position "just happened" to open up in the company that morning in a department that I really wanted to work for. I got the job . . . Start on 6:30 the day after the other job ends . . . Pretty lucky eh? Like I said . . . very interesting and lots of fun too. I drink my lucky elixir every day with my coffee! —E. M.

From the Liquid Luck Meditation: *Say "I am love" . . . feel love, and fill your container with the highest of love for yourself and all of creation.*

Tina Turner sings with considerable angst, "What's love got to do with it?" When the "it" is positive manifestation, everything! I have never met a person in my decades of manifestation work who was excellent at manifesting in a balanced way across all important areas of life including health, financial, career, and friendships, who was not very joyfully and freely loving.

We now come to the high energy we call love. In English we use this word to cover a lot of ground so let's break this down a bit. The ancient Greeks distinguished types of love by using different words for different types of love. They used *Eros* to mean passionate, romantic, and sexual love. Plato felt Eros need not be sexual and therefore we have the term Platonic love for a love between two persons that is very deep but non-sexual. The ancients felt that Eros could be a doorway to appreciation of beauty and spiritual truth.

The word *philia* was used to connote the affectionate warmth found in friendships and is also of course highly treasured as a blessing in life that can lead to many positive experiences. We now use the root of this word to convey great fondness and passion for a subject, as in Francophile (lover of all things French) and audiophile (lover of music). The word *storge* refers to the natural affection in families. *Agape* was considered the highest form of love and involved a spiritual love or a very deep unconditional love. Here love is selfless and expects nothing in return.

The Christian bible gives a sense of the importance of love and the qualities of higher love in 1 Corinthians 13[4] :

> *"If I speak in the tongues of men or of angels, but do not have love, I am only a resounding gong or a clanging cymbal. If I have the gift of prophecy and can fathom all mysteries and all knowledge, and if I have a faith that can move mountains, but do not have love, I am nothing. If I give all I possess to the poor and give over my body to hardship that I may boast, but do not have love, I gain nothing.*

---

4 New International Version (NIV)

Love is patient, love is kind. It does not envy, it does not boast, it is not proud. It does not dishonor others, it is not self-seeking, it is not easily angered, it keeps no record of wrongs. Love does not delight in evil but rejoices with the truth. It always protects, always trusts, always hopes, always perseveres.

Love never fails. But where there are prophecies, they will cease; where there are tongues, they will be stilled; where there is knowledge, it will pass away . . . And now these three remain: faith, hope and love. But the greatest of these is love."

There are many different Hebrew words for love as well, including familial, covenantal, compassionate, friendship, romantic, and neighborly. One of the core commandments of Judaism is, "Love your neighbor as yourself" (Leviticus 19:18). This commandment stands at the center of the central book in the Torah. This implies first valuing oneself in order to be able to share that love with others.

We are spending time elaborating the sense of love that I am referring to because love is so important and is such a misused word. It can be hard to get a sense of what real love is if we have not been exposed to it as children and continue to experience it as adults. Many other things can masquerade as love or come to be equated to love. Co-dependence, being showered with physical or sexual attention, and being given gifts (even with strings attached) can feel like love when we have not experienced love in its purest unconditional forms.

As a therapist I heard countless proclamations of love that were designed to manipulate others, covering the gamut from children being told, "Because I love you I have sacrificed all my own happiness for you, and now you owe me X"; and teenagers and adults being told, "I love you, so you must go to bed with me." I have cringed when I hear statements such as, "I love you so much that I will kill myself and you if I can't be with you." Many of these statements boil down to, "I am so dependent on you that I will be miserable without you or the behavior that I am seeking from you." There are plenty of people, because of their limited background with love, who take these types of statements as a sign of love and then feel the obligation to remain in a toxic relationship. Added to this is that we hear many people gush, "I love this car, or weather, or nacho" when they mean that they really enjoy it.

We must acknowledge the fact that most Western cultures do not cultivate love very well. We start with much less intimate time with mother, compared to cultures where children are breast-fed and carried close to the mother's body for years. We live in isolated nuclear family groups (often now divorced, single parent units), compared to living with extended family. There is little remaining sense of community for most of us. Rugged individualism is applauded versus cooperation. These things serve to diminish our exposure and practice of the type of identity and values that foster love, community, and belongingness. The Chinese select and train children to think anything is possible and to do PK and other psychic skills. They find that children from rural areas are much more likely to demonstrate psychic ability than children from cities. The hypothesis is that city children are more isolated and left-brain dominant, and rural children more in touch with nature and extended family.

We are not talking about the distorted and trivial ways the word love is used. Instead here in this book we are exploring love as a great power that enhances manifestation work and the wisdom to know what to create. This type of love is closest to the Greek agape, an unconditional love that transcends the individual personhood of the lover and the beloved. Most people experience this type love as a feeling that involves openness, warmth, and connection that transcends time and space, a direct connection with beauty, and an elevation of spirit. Included with this feeling is a direct knowingness that is stronger than an intellectual understanding, of the rightness and truth of this type of love.

It may go even deeper than that. My personal feeling is that everything in the universe, physical and non-physical has consciousness. That consciousness creates this time-space illusion/reality paradox. Consciousness appears to be both immanent (the most intimate quality of the individual) and transcendent (spanning all of creation and greater than the sum of all its parts) at the same time.

Consciousness is a paradox much like light being both particle and wave. In the manifestation process at its highest, it may be that we think of something from our identity as particle (individual) and then go to our connection with our nature as wave (unity with all) linking with love to create what we desire. And that at its most essential, consciousness may be synonymous with love. If I am right, love is the most primal and universal energy that exists and underpins all reality. This is why I think that it is the most awesome and effective power that we can tap into when we want to create our world either personally or as a society.

I came to the conclusion, through my psychokinesis work, that consciousness and love at the most basic level of reality may be the same thing. As I mentioned earlier in the book, in 1992 I began to investigate psychokinesis (PK), which is the ability to influence matter through non-physical means. PK can be used to illuminate light bulbs, bend metal and plastic, sprout seeds in your hand, influence computers, dice, and slot machines, and create healing and abundance. PK has been proven at a level of a billion to one by chance in a well-respected body of studies.

I have seen PK in operation in the seventy Inner Vegas Adventures™ that I have trained in the casinos of Las Vegas, where participants journey deeply into personal power. About the only way PK can work is if consciousness indeed creates reality. There are quantum physics explanations of how this may come about. My decades of PK experience also has given me a personal truth that love is the greatest energy from which to do PK (and create your reality) on a consistent and positive basis. Every time I have encountered consciousness in its highest, purest, and most powerful form, it also has been loving. Tapping into love on a very deep level can create miracles of manifestation and healing.

The stories here about Liquid Luck meditation experiences, while amazing, are eclipsed by the events that I have witnessed when people go into an even deeper unconditional love experience in intense workshops such as Manifestation and Creation Squared (MC²) at Monroe Institute, Inner Vegas Adventures™ in Vegas, and SyncCreation® workshops and home study. These have included casino results at up to 1.6 billion to one by chance, instant healings of myriad physical conditions, teleportation of objects, psychic influence over eight thousand miles distance, and many more out-of-the-norm events.

To understand this link between consciousness and love we must expand our belief that consciousness and who we are exists solely in the brain. It is more likely that the brain is actually a transducer that receives and influences consciousness, rather than being the location of consciousness. The word transducer is usually defined as a device that converts one form of energy to another form of energy (much like a radio receiver accepts electromagnetic waves and converts them into sound patterns). Consciousness itself may be independent of the brain and able to exist apart from the brain, and independent of time/space. The large body of PK, remote viewing, telepathy, and energy healing experiments strongly suggest this.

Further there is good evidence that other areas of the body have their own powerful consciousness transducers including the heart, the gut, and the entire human body system. For example, in the book, *New Self, New World*,[5] author Philip Shepherd claims that scientists recognize the web of neurons lining the gastrointestinal tract as an independent brain. He believes that the belly brain is more in touch with life's mysteries than our cerebral brain.

Fascinating as this belly brain is, we are going to focus here more on the consciousness of the heart because it is better studied and more relevant to our discussion about love. Poetry, literature, and common sense have associated the heart with love for millennia. Now science is starting to look

---

5 *New Self, New world: Recovering Our Senses in the Twenty-First Century*, 2010

at this organ, the heart, as more than just an amazingly reliable pumper of blood throughout the biological system.

The Institute of HeartMath is at the spearhead of this research and also leads in developing practical technologies that can help a person enhance the consciousness of the heart. When the emotional heart enters a state of calmness, appreciation, and love, the physical heart demonstrates a very smooth and coherent signal on EKG. Moreover this heart energy projects throughout our bodies and also outward into the world. The research done through HeartMath suggests that this outward projection of heart energy can influence animals and people close by, and may also affect bioelectromagnetic fields, even affecting the world's global fields.

Also of interest here is that HeartMath's research suggests that when we are in a coherent heart energy state, our heart's energy radiates more strongly into the world, and we are more sensitive to detecting information in the fields around us. This may have strong relevance to our topics. My experience is that love energy (the energy of the heart) is the strongest energy from which to do PK, energy healing, and manifestation. This is in line with the findings that the heart energy radiates more strongly into the world when in a coherent state.

We also find that when people are in this state of high love-PK energy, their intuition becomes much stronger, progressing from vague hunches to clear knowings of what will come next on dice or slots, or where and how to send energy for healing, or what step to take next toward an important goal. In this high love state, people experience an increase in synchronicities, revelations, and insights. I started the first chapter with a report of someone solving a complex hardware/

software problem that had eluded solution for two years while in the energy developed with the Liquid Luck meditation. Today I received another report of an inventor who had been stuck for eighteen months on how to develop a whole new way to accomplish his invention's goal. He recently received accurate insight while using Liquid Luck, and his new invention is now in production.

In PK literature there is a body of work spanning decades, called the Global Consciousness Project, which has placed monitors and random number generators around the world. These monitors show that when billions of people focus on one thing such as the 9/11 attack, or even Obama's first acceptance speech, random number generators around the world go from a random signal into an ordered one. These results are again very powerful scientifically, at more than a billion to one by chance. It is one of the strongest proofs that human consciousness effects physical matter reality.

As an example of how wide-ranging HeartMath's research is, I will mention the Global Coherence Initiative.[6] This project is similar in scope to the Global Consciousness Project, but instead of measuring the effects of thought on randomness, the Global Coherence Initiative measures heart energy's effect on the electromagnetic fields of the earth. HeartMath is placing coherence monitors around the world. They have seven in place, currently, that are measuring coherence in the earth's magnetic field. They are finding that when many people around the world meditate in a way that puts their hearts into coherence, the magnetic field of the earth shifts to reflect this coherence.

---

6 http://www.glcoherence.org/

HeartMath, along with finding that heart coherence is related to many positive health and personal outcomes, has developed technologies not only to measure heart coherence but also to help train a person into stronger heart coherence. Their EM-Wave biofeedback device for example can be hooked to a computer where the screen presents a black and white picture of a garden. With a physiologic monitor placed on your ear, as you move into greater heart coherence, the picture gradually adds color, then animals and other beautiful features, giving you real time feedback as to how successful you are at moving into a deeply coherent heart state.

HeartMath has found that even simple exercises, such as putting your hand over your heart, tends to bring your awareness to your heart and helps calm the heart and bring it into coherence. This calmness or coherence can then be further deepened by thinking of a person, animal, or place that you love. Much of what HeartMath does, in my opinion, serves to quiet the ego-mind chatter allowing the physical heart to function better, which allows the feeling and consciousness of the heart to play a greater role in what we are experiencing.

The binaural beat technology in the Liquid Luck meditation can serve this same purpose of bringing the heart's energy and consciousness more into the foreground. Binaural beat technology brings the right and left hemispheres of the brain into balance and this tends to quiet the ego-mind, which is associated with the left hemisphere (past, future, and language focused). This allows the right brain (here/now, unity focused) more voice in our experience of consciousness. This brain balancing and the consequent quieting of the mind also allows us to increase our awareness of the parts of our consciousness that transduce through our hearts and our belly, allowing us to feel our consciousness more completely and as a more unitary whole.

Watching a video of puppies being born or soldiers returning home to joyful reunions with their families can move us into heart space quite easily and we may find ourselves tearful as powerful emotions flow through us. But for most of us this is not very long-lasting. This type of heart opening is more like a cut flower opening, soon to fade. If we become strongly grounded as mentioned earlier in the book, then this heart energy may begin to flow more and more steadily and strongly in our lives.

One of the things that can keep us from fully experiencing love is our tendency to criticize and judge ourselves harshly for our imagined faults. This can include little things such as forgetting someone's birthday, to chronic twinges such as a feeling that we are overweight, to large "screw ups," where we feel badly for a long time afterwards. A heart-helpful affirmation to gentle this judgment energy is as follows. Say to yourself, "Even though I _____(fill in the blank), I completely love and accept myself." Examples might be: "Even though I did not get all my work done, I completely love and accept myself,"; or, "Even though I made a bad decision there, I completely love and accept myself." This affirmation can be said at once whenever you feel self-judgment. I also like to say it at the end of the day, perhaps in the form of, "Even though I was not perfect today, I completely love and accept myself."

In becoming less judgmental about yourself, you may also find yourself more accepting and loving toward others. This is definitely a win-win situation! If the previous affirmation feels like you are coddling yourself too much, remember we do indeed learn better through love than fear. One can (but should not) harshly spank a dog or child and they will likely learn to suppress a behavior out of fear. But if one loves a dog or child, then it is more likely that they will be "good" because it is joyful to be good, and this is self-sustaining. It is the same for you. You will grow, thrive, and become a much better person through love than you will ever become through criticism and fear.

How does love specifically relate to the energies we have explored so far and to manifesting more powerfully in our lives? It is not necessary to be feeling happiness, gratitude, and abundance to feel or experience being loving. We can be loving while in deep grief or depression. That said, it is often much easier to feel loving if we are already feeling happy, abundant, and grateful, so these energies do foster and nurture love. This happens much like a grand cathedral with beautiful architecture and windows fosters prayer. The cathedral or a beautiful spot in nature does not make us pray but creates a conducive energetic environment. Happiness, gratitude, and feeling abundant and compassionate also create a conducive energetic environment for love.

And as we have seen with other energies we are studying, love is part of a magnificent positive feedback cycle. Love elevates and strengthens all these positive energies by wrapping them in a warm blanket of light. Fear tends to cloud and constrain positive energies while love melts fear. Love also promotes the extension of these positive energies, first to ourselves and then outward into the world. The extension allows us to be in communion with the physical world and the world of spirit, and that allows an energetic connection with both worlds, which is necessary for powerful manifestation. These loving energetic connections are how our intent reaches out from the realm of the heart to affect the physical world and bring in what we desire to create.

I will end this chapter by offering a heart-opening exercise to increase love. Take ten to fifteen minutes to do this exercise. It can be a daily meditation or a few times a month—whatever seems right to you. Find a private spot. It can be helpful to be gazing at something beautiful or listening to music that feels heart-opening to you.

First just allow yourself to relax and enter the present moment. When feeling comfortable and in this moment, put your hand on your chest and move your awareness to your heart, feeling the gentle up and down of your chest as you breathe in and out. Now call to mind someone or something that you love deeply. Just let your awareness become completely filled with this memory and allow your heart to relax into feeling fully the love that is flowing. Enjoy this connection with love for a few minutes and then say, "I am Love," and feel more fully your infinite capacity for love. Then let this love flow toward yourself, appreciating your place in this world and also as a spiritual being. End with generously allowing this feeling of love to extend to the world and people around you. As you do this exercise repeatedly, you may well find it becomes easier to enter into deeply loving awareness.

Chapter 6

PRAISE

I have had the Liquid Luck CD for a couple of weeks. I think I listened to it seriously twice in the first 10 days. I work for a non-profit that has been struggling this past year. Last week I attracted a donation of a handicap accessible van worth $35,000! This is the largest single donation our agency has received in 35 years! After I told the director about this, he said to me that the agency had set a goal to raise that same amount for the entire next year! So now I am a hero! On a personal level, I just turned 65 and I just got a notice in the mail from social security that I may be eligible to receive a monthly pension payment from a former employer that I had worked for back in 1992 in the amount of $281/month! This is also totally unexpected! AMAZING! —Steve F.

From the Liquid Luck Meditation: *Now let your heart expand further and join with spirit in joyful praising of all that is, say, "I Praise All" . . . and send this praising energy into your elixir.*

We will now focus on praise in its highest sense. Praise can mean ever more powerful things: to verbally reward a desired behavior, to commend a person or animal for doing what we see as desirable, to applaud someone for doing something that we deeply admire. Here we are using the word praise to mean that we bless, celebrate, and glorify all of creation, seen and unseen. To do so is experienced as deeply joyful, humbling, and exhilarating, and unifies us with all of creation. To do so joins our prayer with the prayers of all other beings of goodwill.

Many feel that the natural state of all consciousness is praise. There is an interesting audio clip that takes the sound of crickets and slows it down as if the cricket lived the equivalent time of a human lifespan. It is called *God's Cricket Chorus* and was created by Jim Wilson and David Carson in 1992. It is available on YouTube.[7] As the sound crickets make slows down, at least on the Wilson/Carson piece, the crickets begin to sound like a hallelujah chorus of sorts, sung by a human choir. There is debate on this piece of "music," that the author altered the sound in some way, and I could not find an author's response to this objection. That said, it is still an interesting piece, suggesting that if we were sensitive enough we might be able to perceive how everything living in nature is praising all of the time. One could also come to this conclusion while gazing at a flower, or witnessing a fabulous sunrise. This is an "All life sings of life" concept.

If one is in a very sensitive and open state when one is expressing praise, it can indeed seem that all of nature is joining in from the sound of wind in the trees, to the sound of the ocean, to bird song and the beauty of a sunset. We sometimes tap into this when our hearts are open when we first fall in love. It can be argued that this state of "infatuation" is a powerful hormone-mitigated, drug-like state. But whatever it is, it serves to open up our perception from the usual ways and makes us feel particularly light, aware, and alive. It is powerful enough to affect judgment, sleep, and appetite.

---

7 https://www.youtube.com/watch?v=uFguHRdUlk8

Some other ways people have tapped into this feeling of praise are: contemplating of the beauty of the physical world, being moved by music, and through deep meditation. I have personally experienced deep praise generated by these triggers and more. For me, when in this state there is a knowing of the rightness of all reality, a sense of the perfect imperfection, a holy glee—meaning a type of joy only available when one is at peace with the world as it is. Yes, from our usual level of perception there is a good deal that is ugly and horrid about the world as it is now. And from that level of reality it is good and ethical to seek to change what we can for the better. Peace is preferred to war, compassion to cruelty. Yet the paradox is that from higher levels of perception there is a knowing that all is in right order.

The original TV series *Star Trek* lasted only three seasons and can be viewed as a fairly corny space cowboy-type show, yet it inspired decades of sequels and movies because it spoke to the deep imprinting we have to be explorers and adventurers. I invite you, if you want to become powerful healers and manifesters to use that explorer's call to delve far into inner space and find this place where the only natural reaction can be to praise with all your soul, joyfully and unendingly, all of creation, whether deemed as hurtful or blissful. This is one of the highest energies that we can experience and I believe aligns us with the angels. For many people this also calls them to praise the creative force behind all of reality that can be named as God or Source.

The call to add praise into our energy elixir comes fairly late in the Liquid Luck meditation because it pulls together the other energies we have focused upon and is the natural result of expanding our feelings of happiness, abundance, gratitude, compassion, and love.

Music has been one of the ways many have captured this feeling of praise. George Frideric Handel wrote the oratorio, *Messiah*, in 1741 and dedicated it to "The Glory of God alone." The Hallelujah from the *Messiah* is one of the most well known of these praise compositions. There are many other works in spiritual, classical, and popular music that use the word, Hallelujah, or Alleluia, to convey this high sense of praise, as in "Praise God" or an expression of ecstatic happiness and gratitude. The hymn *Praise to the Lord, the Almighty* is based on Joachim Neander's *German Chorale* and was published in 1680. It is still popular today. Its opening words are:

Praise to the Lord, the Almighty,
the King of creation!
O my soul, praise Him, for He is thy
health and salvation!

The song, *What a Wonderful World*, originally recorded by Louis Armstrong in 1967, is a good example of a secular praising song from popular music. Beethoven's *Ode to Joy* from his Ninth Symphony captures the joy of praising energy well with wide appeal and speaks of the universal brotherhood of man. There is a YouTube video[8] where 10,000 Japanese people are singing Ode to Joy in German at the same time—pretty impressive! Kids often express praise by jumping up and down, and even adults when faced with unbelievably good news, such as a person beating cancer when expected to

---

8   https://www.youtube.com/watch?v=xBlQZyTF_LY

die, often jump up and down as they proclaim, Alleluia. It is not a mild-mannered word! And praise of this magnitude and depth is not a mild-mannered intellectual experience, rather it is a full body and soul experience.

In the Inner Vegas Adventure workshops in Las Vegas, we meditate using musical pieces that encourage joy, love, the opening the heart, and praising, as a preparation for doing PK and manifesting miracles in our healing circles and in the casino. This works very well, and as the three-day weekend proceeds, repeatedly meditating in this way allows a gradual and gentle but powerful building of these energies to heights many have not experienced before. This is transformative in people's lives.

As mentioned, gratitude is often considered an expression of happiness, yet if we consciously cultivate gratitude, it will produce happiness. Similarly, praise is often thought of as a result of good things happening. Yet in the alchemy of manifestation, if we cultivate praise, this often results in great things happening, turning effect into cause. Praise needs to be genuine. There is even a saying, "Damning with faint praise." But praise can easily be genuine if one takes the time to shift their perspective to "all is in perfect order," where the beauty of the life and the connection to spirit become as real and tangible as anything one might consider rock solid.

Praising Exercise: This exercise comes from the book, *Urban Shaman* by Serge King. While the instructions are fairly simple, it can be challenging in that it can feel strange to do, but it is effective.

- Focus your attention on the present and to the positive.

- Compliment yourself out loud unceasingly for one minute. For example: "I am intelligent and caring. I make terrific lasagna" . . . (that's five seconds worth!)

- Then compliment your immediate environment out loud unceasingly for one minute, as in "This chair is comfortable, I live in a free country, and the woods are beautiful . . . ."

- Notice how you feel before, during, and after doing this. The exercise can bring to awareness issues of worthiness and/or generate feelings of gratitude and love.

When I go into meditation I often strive to reach a deep level of praise consciousness. There, it seems to me that I join with all beings from ants to angels and get swept into a sea of praising energy. It is such a privilege to participate in this universal praising and it is so restorative to body, mind, and soul. In this state of consciousness everything is complete and perfect and anything that I might desire to manifest is the cherry on top of this incredible sundae. There is no thought of scarcity or lack, and manifestation proceeds powerfully and joyfully, with a knowing that "what I desire will manifest . . . or even something better." There is deep trust that this is so and will always be so, and that we will reach our fullest expression of all it can mean to be human, in peace, harmony, and joy. In fact we are already complete within our existence and can see this when we are free of space/time illusion in deep meditation.

A Praising Meditation: This next exercise is designed to help you reach this deep state of praising. In preparation, find something to focus on that inspires praising for you, perhaps some of the music mentioned, or a video of a beautiful nature scene, or sit outside at sunrise or sunset, or in any natural environment that speaks to you of the beauty of the world— even being inside and gazing at a flower will do.

Next relax with a few deep breaths and open your heart and allow yourself to be drawn into the beauty of whatever you are using as a catalyst for this exercise. Then allow your energy to go higher. This is like raising your vibration and becoming more in touch with yourself as spirit while remaining connected to the catalyst you have selected. To do this you might open your hands palms upward and feel as if great light is coming in through your hands and suffusing you with energy. Begin to praise all of creation. You can do this silently or say praising words or even sing and/or dance. Then open your awareness to all beings who are praising at this time and affirm your connection with them and feel the increase in the power of your praising as you join this chorus of praise that spans the world and transcends time and space. Enjoy the praising for as long as you wish and then gently bring yourself back to normal consciousness.

WE HAVE NOW COVERED the energies of happiness, gratitude, abundance, compassion and praise, and the greatest of all—love. At this point in the Liquid Luck meditation the last magic ingredient, luck, is added into this potent brew. Some folks report tingles of excitement when they get to this stage in the meditation. The next chapter introduces the interesting energy of luck.

Chapter 7

LUCK

I received your liquid luck CD and listened that morning. The next day I won a $1,000 scratch-off just by listening to the CD. I couldn't believe the results—awesome! The whole day was fantastic and rewarding. Thanks a bunch. Follow-up: It is still working! Three weeks later I won another $1,000 dollars. Also I won a contest on a local radio station. —Keith F.

From the Liquid Luck Meditation: *And now add the last magic ingredient. Say, "I am lucky" and send all good fortune, synchronicity, and blessing into your potion.*

Just as with the other energies we have been discussing, in order to manifest powerfully and positively we want to bring in the highest and clearest forms of the energy of good fortune. To become consistently lucky most people first need to clear three impediments to the highest of luck energy. These three impediments are any feeling that luck is just a random process; then, any feeling that it is somehow bad to be lucky; and finally, any feeling that you do not deserve to be lucky. That may seem a strange concept that anyone would feel that it is bad to be lucky, but bear with me and you will see what I mean.

First let's look at the idea that luck is a random process. The word, luck sometimes means chance as in "everything is random and at times an infrequent event happens whether good or bad to all of us that we call good or bad luck." Here, luck is considered just a random happening and we really have nothing to do with it in terms of control or influence. Believers in this position feel that "luck is probability taken personally."

There is a problem with deciding that there is no such thing as luck, in the sense of good fortune wherein we may have at least partial influence and control. The decades of psychokinesis studies referred to at the beginning of this book clearly point to things that we usually consider random such as the weather, flips of a coin, and rolls of dice are actually able to be influenced by human consciousness. Also, some people have something happen that is so lucky that it defies all reasonable attempts to explain it away by chance, such as winning a major lottery five times. This should not happen by chance even one in a quadrillion times.

Then there seems to be life-long patterns that defy chance. A percentage of us seem to be lucky very consistently throughout life and some people are amazingly unlucky. Roy Sullivan was struck by lightning seven times over a thirty-five-year period. The odds of being struck by lightning for a person over the period of eighty years have been roughly estimated as one in 10,000. If the lightning strikes were random, the probability of being hit seven times would be 1 in 10 to the 28th power—ten followed by 28 zeros.

Sometimes it is hard to say whether we have been lucky or unlucky. Here is a story from *Today I found Out*.[9]

---

9 http://www.todayifoundout.com/index.php/2013/10/man-cheated-death-seven-times-went-win-lottery/

Frane Selak, avoided death seven times but was often injured in accidents that killed others with him and that should have killed him as well: a train he was in jumped the tracks and plunged into an icy river killing seventeen people, a plane door burst open killing nineteen people and he landed in a hay stack, a bus went into a river drowning four others, his car burst into flames twice, while he was walking he was hit by a bus, and another time his car plunged down a 300-foot embankment. Then he won a million dollar lotto. While people nicknamed him "The Luckiest Man in the World," for cheating death so many times and winning the lottery, Selak disagrees. "I never thought I was lucky to survive all my brushes with death. I thought I was unlucky to be in them in the first place . . . ."

Often what looks like luck may be preparation meeting opportunity, and then the guts to take a well-understood risk. But I do think that there is genuine luck, meaning that the universe, angels, God, or another person basically reaches out and blesses you with good fortune. This good fortune may be as simple as a smile, an encouragement, or guidance coming at just the right time and in just the perfect way. It can be as big as winning the lottery when you have huge medical bills, are out of work, and are sinking into despair. I think that the best way to invite this kind of luck or blessing into one's life is to feel deserving of it, to trust that it exists, to ask for it, and to allow it to come to you. My butt has been saved many times by this kind of blessing. And it is also true that wondrous things beyond my imagining have come via this kind of blessing. I love this saying which is purported to be an ancient Afghan proverb: "If luck is with thee, why hurry? If luck is against thee, why hurry?"

In decades of teaching manifestation and particularly in the seventy Inner Vegas Adventure workshops, I have found that people most often report feeling lucky before they win and then this luck is confirmed by the win versus feeling flat before the win and lucky after the win. There is a particular feeling and belief state associated with the generation of luck.

Here is a personal example of the opposite of feeling lucky from my book *Inner Vegas*—it embodies the idea that it is bad to be lucky or to put it in another way—that true and lasting good only comes from hard work. A long time ago, after I had rolled well many times in Vegas, when I would approach the table, the crew would announce, "Here comes Mister Lucky, bet big now, he is a super hot roller!" This would immediately put me into self-consciousness and fear of failure, and I would often lose quickly. The next time I went to the tables the dealers didn't even have to greet me as "Mr. Lucky" to throw me off my game. All I needed to do was fear that they would say it and I would allow that fear to put a big crimp in my energy before I even started to play. I could have used their Mister Lucky statement as encouragement to bolster my confidence, but that was not how I was built. My training was that if someone praised you, you should act modestly and deflect the attention immediately.

Just to show you how sticky to the ego two words can be, and to illustrate how it might come to be that one would feel it is bad to be lucky, I am going to go a bit deeper with "Mr.

Lucky." In my family I was the youngest of four boys. By the time I came along my parents were considerably more affluent and considerably mellower about rules such as curfew. My memory of events is that my brothers would tease me about being the lucky one, whereas they were the hard-working ones who had experienced much stricter parenting. This would often come up when I was petitioning my parents for some favor that I really wanted. And my brothers' teasing threatened my being granted the favor because it increased my parents' reluctance to grant my request. My parents wanted to treat all their children equally. So when they heard, "You never let us do that when we were his age," it gave them pause. I would rebel against this description, saying to my brothers and to myself with vehemence, "I am not lucky." I probably even stamped my feet for emphasis. I attempted to counter their perception by working hard at everything from schoolwork to chores, so I developed a strongly set pattern of working hard.

Now here I was thirty years later being called Mr. Lucky, just when I wanted to be lucky as I began a PK run at the casino tables. As they say, this really screwed with my Chi! The bigger issue of always working hard had to be addressed continually while learning PK. I definitely had a tendency to make this playful, trusting, and joyous activity into hard work. Just to be clear, I do indeed feel very fortunate and have tremendous gratitude for my blessings and am happy now to say that I am lucky. But for a long time there was an ego part of me that was not comfortable when someone else called me lucky. And that ego part felt that hard work should be admired much more than luck. While I felt this way, I was not able to get any royal flushes in video poker despite trying for twenty years. Since that time I have cleared this belief and began to feel that it was okay to be lucky. I have enjoyed receiving six royal flushes (at 40,000 to one by chance each) in the past five years, despite playing at the slots less often than chance would predict these results.

The latest royal flush came a week ago while I was relaxing after training an Inner Vegas Adventure workshop. I am going to go into detail here because it can give you a taste of the types of energy conducive to luck. I was feeling very happy with the workshop and fortunate that the participants were so caring and had experienced a great time, as it had been a very stressful week for me personally just before the workshop.

I was also in a very open-hearted state, as my brother John had died in a beautiful and peaceful way the week before. He died at home with his wife, my wife, and me holding him and sending him energy and light and talking to him gently as he passed away peacefully. It was a situation where he could have been struggling for days for breath. He passed just after we played one of his favorite songs for him. This was a profoundly sacred experience for me. The week before I had received a message from a highly intuitive channeler. She said that my brother Peter (who had committed suicide more than twenty years ago) was helping John's transition from the other side and that Peter was going to try to arrange it so that I could be home and with John when it happened, as Peter felt that the isolation of his own death was not ideal. For me to be home was a challenge in that my travel schedule often takes me away from home about every other week.

I left for this Vegas workshop the day after my brother John's funeral. My wife had a psychic reading right before we arrived in Vegas for the workshop and her psychic without knowing the details about John's death, asked, "Did you, Joe, and John's wife have your hands on John as he passed"? He said that John felt great light and love coming through our hands and it helped him transition easily and with so much good energy that he was immediately well ahead in his transition progress compared to most who die.

With this profound experience resonating though my consciousness and heart, and the relief of delivering a quality workshop under challenging circumstances, I went to one of my favorite poker machines to relax. I recalled the feeling of being in the cascade of my abundance waterfall, having just listened to my new Abundance Waterfall CD the day before. Within minutes, I hit my royal flush. Since it was late at night, after I was paid I attempted to sleep but could not (too excited) so I went back down to the casino and hit a progressive four-of-a-kind on my third pull, and followed it by the same win again two pulls later. All-in-all a $5,000 night and then I could go to sleep. I felt my Mom's presence right before the win, suggesting that if we are open to it we may indeed receive lucky help from the other side at times.

I do not think I am alone in my struggle to understand the appropriate place of luck in our lives. When Americans are surveyed they believe most success is based upon hard work. When we have done really well at something, do we not prefer to be told that we have worked hard and deserve it, versus that we are lucky? We like this illusion that hard work is all that is needed; then things feel more under our control and we can feel that we are doing better than someone else because we deserve it due to our hard work.

Yes, we should be inspired by people rising from disadvantaged circumstances and applaud their dedication to a goal. Yet it is good to have the humility to understand that luck may also have something to do with success or failure as well. This will deepen our compassion toward ourselves and others when things go poorly and increase our gratitude when things go well. As we learn to influence our circumstances, we might even be able to increase our luck. If we acknowledge the role of luck in our lives, then we can understand what it is and cultivate good luck's presence in our lives. And if we over-value hard work as a moral pinnacle, then, as we create our reality, we probably will create a lot of hard work for ourselves!

One of the prevailing myths in western culture is that we live in a meritocracy wherein people get what they deserve based upon merit. We make those who have achieved fame in sports and business into heroes. And we like to think that they got to the pinnacle solely through hard work, smarts, courage, and dedication. The facts are different—yes, most of them embody these qualities, but also there has been a good bit of luck. One example is that to have the best shot at the top, when you are born has a lot to with it, and we have no control over the timing of this important event. It turns out, as demonstrated in Malcolm Gladwell's book, *Outliers: The Story of Success*, that the exact month you are born determines when you start school and some kids get to start nearly a full year chronologically older than other children; and these kids, because they are more physically and developmentally advanced, get picked for sports team, get better marks, and are put in better classes simply because they are more advanced due to their age.

Most of the people reading this book are lucky not to be among the nearly one billion people who are starving or the over one billion people who live in extreme poverty on this planet. Most are lucky to be living in a place of peace—not war—to have parents that were at least adequate enough to keep them alive, and that they are living in a free country that has some respect for human rights and holds opportunities for bettering one's condition. It is also fortunate that we live in a time of rapid and spectacular change in many fields including medicine, the arts, technology, and communication, and a time of decreasing war, starvation, and infectious disease. I am old enough to remember kids my age who contracted polio. Is it not lucky to know that an iron lung is not part of your or your children's future?

Here is a list of things that we do not earn, that we have no conscious control over (at least from a perspective of life here—karmic and other contracts possibly chosen from the other-side are not addressed here). We do not consciously control exactly when, where, and to whom we are born. Would you not agree that is good to be lucky at least in these very important determinants of the type of life we will be living? Further, it is fairly easy to see that it is lucky to be blessed with parents, siblings, extended family, and community who are nurturing, and who have the ability to provide beyond the basics, have access to good medical care and sanitation, and perhaps even have strong social networks to ease our way into academic and business settings, and facilitate us finding suitable partners? Most of the people reading this book have been lucky to experience life and its opportunities very differently than a child born into the ghettos that surround many of our major cities.

If your life situation from birth till now was like a random hand of cards, would you trade your hand for someone's else's on the planet without knowing what the new cards would be, when one of eight people are starving? If not, then I think it is appropriate to consider yourself lucky to have the life cards that you now have. We have mentioned the Law of Attraction that like attracts like, so if you want to be lucky, it is good to feel lucky and to feel that to be lucky is a good thing. It is helpful to understand that luck can be just as useful and valuable as the capability to do hard work.

I went into a lot of elaboration here intentionally. If, as you read these statistics about how many are struggling with disadvantaged circumstances, instead of feeling lucky, you felt guilt for your own good fortune, this next section is just for you!

Now it is time to focus on the third possible impediment to consistent good fortune—any feeling, however subtle, that you don't deserve to be lucky, and its variants such as everybody is lucky but me; nothing lucky ever happens to me; being jealous or resentful of another person's luck; and feeling guilty for being luckier than someone else. It is important to understand that in an abundant universe, you being lucky does not take away from anyone's else's ability to receive good fortune. In fact it just might inspire them to receive greater blessings. And with good fortune, you then have the wherewith-all to help others more effectively. And, of course, their luck does not detract from your luck potential either.

I have been on many radio shows where someone calls in claiming to be one of the most unlucky people in the world. I respond compassionately and offer the observation that it is seldom about a lack of deservingness or lack of value, but

rather about fears and limiting beliefs that are usually generated by our life experience so far. I also say, Great! If life for
most people contains a random mix of good and bad and
you are experiencing mostly bad, then you are influencing the
randomness quite powerfully by doing negative PK, if you
will. Now all you need to do is remove some limiting beliefs
and fears, and it will flip to positive PK; what seems like bad
luck will flip to good luck, and you could become a powerful
manifester of great experiences.

Why would a person feel that they don't deserve to be
lucky? One way is to feel guilt, because guilt dictates that we do
not deserve to be blessed and in fact we deserve the opposite,
to be punished for some real or imagined failure on our part.
To address this issue I will present a modification of an exercise
that is included in my SyncCreation® Home Study Manifestation Course on a special meditation CD, called Abundance
Tree. Even without the CD, you can do this exercise at home
and I think you will find it quite powerful in clearing impediments to greater luck. The exercise came to me in full detail
during a dream, when I had asked before falling asleep for a
healing of anything in the way of greater abundance.

The Abundance Tree Exercise

This exercise is designed to help eliminate unconscious blocks
to abundance, whether in the form of feelings or limiting
thoughts. It is an energy conversion exercise. Find a quiet
hour. Bring a couple of pieces of paper and a pencil with you.
Relax, and ask for help from highest source and your own
unconscious as you do this exercise. Now list one item per
line, in a 1-2-3 fashion, any ways past or present that you have

felt guilt for acts and thoughts, large or small. This can also be guilt for things that you did not do but that you feel you should have done. We do this exercise because guilt creates an "I don't deserve blessings" pattern, which blocks good coming to you. List anything that comes to mind even if it seems trivial—no judgment, just observe with compassion and put it down if it comes into your awareness. List things as minor as not going to church on Sunday (or synagogue on Saturday), or forgetting someone's birthday, to times when you hurt or failed another or yourself in a major way. When you feel the energy slacken, begin writing with your non-dominant hand and see if more items flow through in this manner.

Now continue this list with any way you have felt or feel unlucky, again putting on paper anything that comes to your mind without regard to the objectivity of the item, because if a part of you feels that the item is an example of your being unlucky, it can impair your sense of good luck.

When this listing feels complete, take the list and the pencil with you to a place where you can be comfortable, for example in a recliner or on a bed. Then close your eyes for a few moments, relax even further and imagine yourself in a beautiful field or meadow of soft grass, with the sun warming your body, as a nice breeze keeps you refreshed. Close by is a tree symbolizing your abundance. This is your abundance tree, strong in structure and ready to receive nutrients. Nearby is also a pile of dead branches. See each item on your list as an individual branch in the pile. Each branch represents the pattern of frozen energy that is created by having that particular guilt or sense of unluckiness. Energy is in fact neutral and you can now release this energy by breaking apart the pattern holding it in a negative form of feeling guilt or unluckiness.

Now imagine a large wood chipper, like tree-cutting crews use for clean up (those noisy machines with sharp rotating blades and a big chute, out of which spew wood chips which can be used as a fertilizing mulch). Turn on the wood chipper, hear its powerful whine, and feed into it, one branch at a time, the pile of branches at your feet, crossing each item off your list as you go. Hear the tone of the machine change and then return to its strong whine after each branch goes through. It works even better to make the sound of the wood chipper, letting your voice change as the branches go through. Smell the woody freshness of the released energy. When you have finished with the whole pile, turn off the chipper. Rest a moment, then take the resulting pile of fresh, nutrient laden, wood-chips and spread them all around the base of your abundance tree. See the tree greening and growing fully healthy, with strong roots that reach deep into the earth and a crown that reaches to the heavens. Enjoy your refreshed abundance tree for as long as you like. Then bring yourself back to an awake and alert state. Throw away or burn your list, letting go once and for all of the constriction and pain represented by the list.

WE HAVE NOW COVERED all the important energies that go in the making of the energy potion, Liquid Luck, and that I consider essential for creating a life pattern of consistent good fortune and abundance. We have seen how grounding, happiness, gratitude, and feeling abundant, compassionate, praising, loving, and fortunate all work together synergistically, resulting in a powerful flow of energy that can be used toward creating the best that life can offer. We have been able to cover these areas in detail in a way that could not be done in the thirty-seven minute Liquid Luck meditation. Along the way, hopefully your understanding of these important energies and the process of manifestation has deepened. I have also attempted to provide practical and enjoyable exercises to practice at home to expand these energies in your own life. If you have just read about the exercises up to this point, I strongly suggest that you experience the exercises yourself. If there seems too many of them, just select one or two to start with that intuitively call to you. Then do the one that you feel the most resistance toward doing because that one will often be the most transformational.

I will finish this chapter by mentioning a song that helps me enter that zone where I feel lucky: KD Lang's *Luck in My Eye*.[10] Good Luck!

10 http://www.youtube.com/watch?v=mX5D3DkVDwg

Chapter 8

SYNCHRONICITY, SERENDIPITY, TIMING, AND TRUST

I listened to Liquid Luck on a loop last night, woke this morning and it was still playing through my headphones, went to a retail show as I have a design company. A fellow exhibitor parked right next to me and I spoke to him about "losing £300 worth of stock in a box two weeks earlier and that I thought was stolen." Low and behold , the very same guy had picked it up. Because the box was plain he had no idea it was mine and was going to see who sold this product at the show today and ask them, "Did you leave anything"? That's a little bit surreal and it would appear synchronicity and maybe your Liquid Luck may be connected? Anyway thanks for the reply and I will be listening again tonight as it's a £110 million rollover on the UK lottery, fingers crossed. Thanks. —Steve

There are a few more areas that I will cover in the next chapters that I consider important. First, however I want to be sure that some words and concepts used after the potion is created are clear in their meaning and explore how they are related to the energies of grounding, happiness, gratitude, abundance, compassion, praise, love and good fortune that we have focused upon so far. These are the concepts of synchronicity, serendipity, timing, and trust. They appear in the Liquid Luck meditation as follows:

From the Liquid Luck Meditation: *This potion, when swallowed, brings the drinker a day where everything fortuitously falls in place for great benefit. On this day—synchronicity, serendipity, grace, and positive energy abound, bringing you easily and joyfully to your highest good and desire. This potion brings the clarity to notice just the right thing at the right time . . . the impulse to move with just the right timing in the right direction . . . and the courage to act on these intuitions with great trust. This is an excellent potion to use whenever you desire help to achieve your goal . . . or even something better!*

When the energies we have been exploring have all been purified and heightened, then the magic begins where synchronicity and serendipity abound!

Synchronicity is a very interesting phenomenon. Meg Lundstrom has a great and simple definition of synchronicity. She calls it "a wink from the cosmos." A more extensive definition might be that synchronicity is a sequence of events that appear meaningfully related when no clear causal relationship exists. It is the idea of a meaningful coincidence or a coinciding of events unlikely to appear together. And this coinciding can result in a range of feelings and results from experiencing delight and surprise, all the way to the synchronicity having life-changing impact on a person. Many see synchronicity as a confirming sign that they are proceeding in the right direction in their thinking or actions. Most students of synchronicity feel that events can be connected by meaning, just as they might be connected by cause and effect.

Synchronistic events suggest an underlying pattern that is grander than the visible reality wherein the synchronicity appears. Carl Gustav Jung who developed the theory of a Universal Mind, or Collective Unconscious coined the term synchronicity to describe "temporally coincident occurrences of acausal (non-cause-effect) events." Following discussions with Albert Einstein, Jung believed that there were parallels between synchronicity and aspects of relativity theory and quantum mechanics. From the religious perspective, synchronicity shares similar characteristics to the concept of grace. Synchronicities can shift a person's preoccupation with their own self toward an awareness that they a part of a magnificent and mysterious whole.

In his book, *Synchronicity* (1952), Jung relates a synchronistic event with a patient who was overly wedded to rational thinking and out of touch with the more magical part of life. He was sitting opposite her one day, listening to her. She had a dream the night before in which someone had given her a golden scarab. While she was still telling him this dream, he heard something gently tapping on the window. He turned around and saw an insect against the windowpane. He opened the window and caught the insect in the air as it flew in. It was a beetle, whose gold-green color resembled that of a golden scarab. He handed the beetle to her with the words, "Here is your scarab." This experience punctured her rationalism and broke the ice of her intellectual resistance.

From *Catching the Bug of Synchronicity*[11]: "Synchronicities are those moments of "meaningful coincidence" when the boundary dissolves between the inner and the outer. At the synchronistic moment . . . our internal, subjective state

---

11 http://www.awakeninthedream.com/wordpress/catching-the-bug-of-synchronicity/

appears, as if materialized in . . . the outside world. Touching the heart of our being, synchronicities are moments in time in which there is a fissure in the fabric of what we have taken for reality and there is a bleed-through from a higher dimension outside of time. Synchronicities are expressions of the dreamlike nature of reality, as they are moments . . . when the timeless, dreamlike nature of the universe shines forth its radiance and openly reveals itself to us . . . ."

Most of us have had occasional synchronicities. It is likely that many were just a delightful surprise, others a sign of confirmation, and perhaps some that were life changing. For me the meeting and courtship of Elena, who became my wife, was filled with many synchronicities. When energy is raised high and hearts are open in the Inner Vegas Adventure workshops and the SyncCreation workshops, as well as in many of the Monroe Institute programs, we see a dramatic increase in the number and quality of synchronicities that people experience. People report that when they think of someone they need to talk with, the person appears in moments. They relate that the person they sit next to "randomly" at dinner or who joins them in the elevator is just the right person at the right time to give them insight, wisdom, or support. They have their elevator get stuck on floor nine and then go to the casino bet the number nine and win big.

Over the years of my doing this work, synchronicities have expanded in quantity and quality, so they now occur on a regular basis. I have come to feel that they are a constant reminder of being supported by our magical universe. And such synchronicities can in fact be shaped by our intent, both to experience more of them, and as to their content. When I am starting a project, I now open to synchronicity. I trust and expect that many will happen that will help me in ways that I do not even know I need help. They make my progress toward my goal a more delightful, meaningful, and easy path. Also, many of the synchronicities will take the form of clear signs that I can use to guide my path. For example, I often see a feather (even at night falling from the sky) when I am getting a strong "yes" from the universe.

Our discussion of synchronicity leads us to the term serendipity, which can mean both good fortune as in a happy coincidence and also an aptitude for making desirable discoveries by accident. The term was first coined in the 1700s from the Persian fairy tale, *The Three Princes of Serendip*, whose heroes were always making fortuitous discoveries by accident. It is often now used to describe scientific discoveries, such as for penicillin, where the investigator was not looking for what he discovered. Serendipity also implies that the person experiencing them is wise enough to link together or take advantage of things that may appear random to another person. I find this to be true—our ego-mind tends to lock us into a habitual way of thinking, which often results in us going through the world with perceptual and intellectual blinders on. When we raise our energy and open our hearts, thereby softening the ego, then we are much more likely to call in synchronicities, but also be able to see and utilize serendipity.

Part of the delight of this open-hearted, high energy way of living is that our timing tends to become more impeccable which allows the synchronicities and serendipities to occur that will lead us to our dreams in ways better and more quickly than we can imagine. And the journey toward our goal is often enriched by experiences and people along the way that could not have been anticipated as we started on our path. When we are open-hearted and feeling connected to other people and the world (grounded) we tend to be able to read the signs better, in terms of not only how but also when to proceed. We call the person at just the right time to reach them when they are available and in a very receptive mood. We read just the right book at the right time. In fact, the opposite is also true. When we seem to be struggling, meeting road blocks at every turn and our timing is off, then that is a clear sign that either one of two things may be occurring. One is that it is not the right path or time; or two, that we are not in the correct energy for what we are attempting to accomplish. If you find yourself in this position, it is a great time to use some of the exercises in this book to reset your energy.

It is interesting to me that in many dictionaries the word immediately following serendipity is "serene" because that brings up the next important aspect to generating great luck, and that is trust. All we have explored in this book points out to me that it is not a hostile world unless we make it so for ourselves both individually and as a culture. Rather, our earth experience is designed so that it can be a beautiful experience filled with love despite and perhaps because of the challenges physical life presents. It is very difficult to trust when you have had the experience of much ongoing pain, but those who cultivate trust using whatever philosophical or other tools they can manage, often begin to experience the sweetness of life to a much greater degree. This generates even more trust that this is a good world and that they are a good person. It forms a very positive feedback cycle, where the more you trust in goodness, the more goodness appears, and the more you trust, because you keep receiving confirmation that your trust is merited. Jimmy Burgess in *One Decision Can Change Everything* puts it this way: "*Are you going to allow your current struggle or painful past to make you bitter or better?*"

Sometimes being willing to more deeply trust involves surrender when things have not been going well, and even if they have gone well, that circumstances will continue to nurture you. It helped me to surrender when I decided that instead of viewing surrender as giving up, that when I surrender all I am really surrendering is my illusion of separateness.

Through this book and through any other ways that show up to grace your life, I hope that you move into a life where happiness, gratitude, abundance, love, and luck abound. And that you experience the joy and power of this, and the delight of sharing this with others. Sometimes life flows easily when applying the principles that have been presented. At other times there are dragons that must be fought. The next chapter will discuss these dragons a bit in the effort to help when things are not as smooth and easy as we would like them to be.

Chapter 9

DRAGONS GUARDING TREASURE

Within an hour or two of listening to Liquid Luck for the first time on a walk with my dog about a week ago, I received a phone call out of the blue telling me that I had over two thousand dollars in unclaimed property (a tax refund) from a state where our family had resided briefly about 15 years earlier. I confirmed it on the state treasury's website and have filed my claim for the refund. I have never received such a call before, or anything like it. In my view, this was no coincidence. Since then, I have enjoyed my sips of liquid luck each and every morning and so far my luck is holding! Thanks, Joe!

We have covered many dynamic principles of creating good fortune and abundance. Following these principles can result in enhanced health, family and friend relationships, business opportunities, finances, and in an increase of synchronicity, great timing, and support as you create your dreams. However this abundance work does not always go smoothly—that is what makes it interesting! When the going gets tough, attempting to create abundance becomes a wonderful classroom, a learning path toward greater self-understanding and spiritual development.

When I was progressing along my own path, I found many unexpected challenges, which I came to call my dragons because in myth dragons guard treasure. And I see being able to do PK, applying energy healing, and manifesting what I desire as great treasures, indeed. Fighting many dragons was hard and confusing work. It was similar to fighting brush fires where I would no sooner put one out and another would smoke, then flame. Some of the dragons that popped up regularly were self-judging and self-depreciating thoughts. At other times the dragon would take the form of a person or organization that seemed "out to get me," in terms of frustrating my progress toward my goal. Often the dragon would appear as a negative emotion. And many times it appeared as a belief that limited my progress or restricted what I felt I was entitled to wish for or what was possible to accomplish.

The first major step for me was to understand that I was actually fighting only one multi-headed dragon, called fear. No matter what form that dragon's head would take, I found it could always be traced back to fear. This made complete sense, because it appears true that the main driving power behind positive manifestation progress is love, and also true that fear clouds love's ability to be felt, to be expressed, and to shine. Fear wrenches one out of the present moment and into dwelling on the past or worrying about the future, and we know that the power place for manifestation is in the now present moment. Fear also threatens grounding and balance by moving us out of strong connection with our bodies, hearts, and spirits, and into our heads as we try to calculate how to hide from or protect ourselves from what is feared.

In my view, we all manifest our reality all of the time but it is often weak (because of lack of clarity or conflicts in what we desire) or unconscious, or quite often negative due to fear. When we are in positive creative space a person, place, thing, or event will come along to reflect our positivity to us and help us toward our goal. When we are in negative space, it is also true that a person, place, thing, or event will show up presenting us with the opportunity to identify, face, and then transform our fear. Unfortunately, we often miss this opportunity by going into victim energy and feeling that the person (place, thing, event) who shows up is a bad person for messing with or frustrating us.

Bullying is clearly an unwelcome and damaging behavior, but when we look at this situation, we often treat the person being bullied only as an innocent victim, and ignore that the person being bullied may have fear and a poor self-concept to begin with, which tends to invite bullying. I bring up the issue of bullying because it points to how we hold the victim energy as almost sacred, in the sense that while most of us know that most of the time there are two sides to every story, we are never supposed to question the guiltlessness of the victim position. Often the bullying might be based on something outside the person's control such as race or sexual orientation. Of course no one deserves to be bullied for any reason. This is not the same as blaming the victim, but from our position of deciding to take more conscious control over our manifesting, as adults we must also seek areas of self-responsibility (ability to respond) for situations wherein we feel victimized.

From my decades of casino play, I can almost guarantee that if I am in fear while playing, some individual will come up that concretizes my fear. It may be a person who is betting big and betting against me, or a cigar smoker blowing smoke in my face and disrupting my concentration and attempts to be in a good mood; or the crew at the tables will be sullen and make mistakes in my payouts, etc. I might also have trouble finding a parking space, or a table at which to play—someone or something blocks me—and invites me to find and face my fear. This is also true in business or relationships—when there is fear, it will manifest as blocks, setbacks, or frustrations.

In fact the stronger our commitment becomes to be conscious manifesters, the more likely that any positive *or negative* thought or emotion will manifest a result more clearly and quickly. Given this, I often affirm, "Small lessons please, I am willing to pay attention." And also that, "I am willing to learn through pleasure, delight, and success." It is tempting to pay more attention to things that cause us pain than pleasure. If we let this natural tendency rule, then we tempt our guidance system to send us painful experiences when it needs to get our attention. And if the lesson is really important for our growth and we keep ignoring the smaller lessons and signs, the universe or our own spirit tends to slowly escalate our experiences until we have to face them, and by then it may become very unpleasant. Our guidance system operates much more pleasantly if we really pay close attention to any of the good things we may have helped create, give gratitude for them, and assess why they happened.

As one begins the journey of becoming a conscious creator of one's reality, it is likely that there will be some signs that this stuff really works, small successes at least. Then there will often be fears surfacing and manifesting in the form of people or events. I think that this is because we have tendencies (or fears) to not want to become too different than our families or friends, and we might have concerns about power and its abuse, and finally we just tend to fear change itself because it contains the unknown. When we move into a much different relationship and responsibility concerning our reality, things do change.

So let's be clear. In my opinion, we live in a highly dynamic, interactive, and conscious universe. The world does not conspire against you, me, or anyone. Rather, in conspires with you to create a reality reflective of your thinking and feeling. This can be very challenging in that there are entire cultures, and definitely family trees that appear to have come here to play out this drama starting from a very negative and victim perspective. It can be extremely difficult to swim again this sea of limits and negativity. Also if one has had decades of painful and suppressive experiences, it is challenging to change the pattern.

I have seen this close at hand in my own thirty-year depression, my brother's suicide, and my three decades of work with psychotherapy clients. The response to all this pain should definitely be deep compassion. But sometimes the most compassionate thing to do is yell, "WAKE UP! It doesn't have to be this hard! There are resources that can help you and if you want I can help you find them." As adults, we do have a choice. Victor Frankl[12] and many others even found a way in the midst of concentration camps to rise from the worst of situations to dignity and meaning. People have risen out of ghettos, war scenes, abusive and neglectful families, and have even broken the golden handcuffs of great but stifling wealth and privilege, to become truer to themselves and their amazing capacities as human beings.

---

12 Victor Frankel, *Man's Search for Meaning.*

When I was developing the meditation, Liquid Luck, I was well aware of the many-headed dragon of fear. Because of the purpose and length of the meditation experience, I decided that it was best not to stimulate and confront this dragon directly. Rather, in my manifestation work I had found that one could sing this dragon to sleep and gently bypass it, in order to get some excellent manifestation work done. And the most effective song for calming dragons to sleep is the song of love. So in Liquid Luck, there is the focus on all the positive energies that we have mentioned and no direct mention of fear. This is because the meditation is designed to give a person a really good taste of the process of creating the miracle of manifestation and that this process can work quickly for them.

Chapter 10

TALES OF TREASURE

I just wanted to let you know about my positive experience with Liquid Luck. When I first received it, I had set up my stereo to replay repeatedly. I had it ready in the morning. When first awakening, I would put on headphones and stay in bed and let it play till I had to get going so it would play one or two times and I did it thirty days in a row. The first week I found five dollars three times. I'm in sales and I had my best month in a couple of years and led a national company in sales, so my income doubled. And the icing on the cake was that I'm huge fan of Jeff Beck. He is a private person and hard to meet. I've been trying for years and I got to meet him and Brian Wilson, so it was a great thirty-day run. Thanks! —A.G.

As you have seen, I have included a manifestation story in the person's own words at the beginning of each chapter. For this purpose I used reports that were brief. I would like to now present more stories of people's success including some longer ones. I think that all these stories taken together give a great feel for the process of manifestation, using Liquid Luck and its principles to achieve quick success. Note that most of them include the writer reporting surprise and delight. When most people first attempt this process, they are often very unsure that it can work, so being pleasantly surprised is natural.

Perhaps even more interesting is when the people I work with stay in touch over many years, even a decade after seeing their first results, they still report surprise and delight at each occurrence of manifestation. I have found this to be true in my own experience as well. This work remains terrific fun even in the long term. It is like the experienced golfer still getting excited at the perfect shot. When you nail it, it feels great!

And much like in sports or the arts, in manifestation work there always seems to be room for improvement if the activity ignites your passion. Continued work on these skills satisfies our desire to explore more of what our potential may really be. In addition to becoming more skillful, there is the reward of increased life enrichment from expanding our ability to love, to be compassionate, and to feel abundant because, as we have seen, this results in a more joyful life.

As time goes on most of the people that I keep in touch with in this work flower into receiving as much or more joy out of helping others as they do from manifesting for themselves. They begin to share their financial abundance more and more freely, but also their time, attention, and energy in service of others. When I have the good fortune to see them at workshops over the years, each time is like a snapshot in which they often appear a bit younger, with more smile in their eyes, and they seem both more gentle and more powerful. But mainly they become more sensitive and responsive to other's needs as time goes on. Here are some more stories, mostly from people at the beginning of their abundance journeys as they try out the Liquid Luck meditation. I edited only for clarity. I hope you enjoy them.

After using Liquid Luck I won a raffle at the Accordion Fest last weekend. I won the prize I wanted. A quilt made with previous festival t-shirts. There were 2500 tickets and about 8 or 10 winners. I am stoked! Thanks. —B. V.

I had numerous turns of luck in only 24-hours. It absolutely floored me. Here they are: Just Pull Over! I put it on my iPod and was listening to Liquid Luck on my way to class* (I am a university professor.) The brief sample was wonderful to listen to. Just those few seconds made me happy and relaxed. I continued the drive to work, which became annoying as I was behind a person going very slowly. It was driving me nuts. My biggest flaw is that I am an impatient person. As I was alone in my car, I said to no one in particular, "Would you please just pull over?" To my amazement, the car immediately pulled over and let me past. I continued down the road and about 10 minutes later, was again behind a slow driver. I laughed and said, "Hey, how about you pull over, too!" The car pulled over. At this point I began to get a little unnerved. I said once OK, but twice? That's a little weird. Next up was a town truck carrying asphalt to repair potholes in the streets. They are horrendously slow. I said, "Wonder if there's any chance . . .?" and the truck turned right. I continued on my way to school and got to one area where there is always a long traffic backup. As long as I have been driving this route, there has never been a time when there wasn't traffic. I almost fainted when I pulled onto *that stretch of the road and there was not one car. Not a single one. I zipped along and of course when I got to school, a parking space opened up just as I pulled into the lot. It is not easy to find a parking space at just about any campus—I'm sure you know that.*

The next morning, I was driving home from taking my spouse to the airport. I found a beautiful metal trellis set out by the side of the road. It was seven feet tall and was quite ornate. Someone was throwing it out. It was in very good condition. To buy something like this would be around $600-700, minimum. I had long wanted a decorative piece like this for my house, as I am an avid gardener. I went home and got my station wagon and returned: It was still there. I put it in my wagon and took it home. I was happy about my find, but thought I would have to paint it. As soon as I put it in place, I could see the color was perfect for the garden spot I had chosen. The piece looks stunning! I am so incredibly happy to have it.

But something else happened on the trellises. I was working outside late this afternoon and my neighbor came over with his dog, who I love. He asked, "Can she hang around with you for awhile?" I said sure and that I was planning to be working outside for a couple hours. He then said, "Beautiful trellises. They were yours by one minute." I looked at him quizzically. He said he had spotted them while he was out in his sports car (two-seater). He, too, raced home for an appropriate vehicle with which to transport them. When he drove back to the trellises, however, he saw me loading them up in my wagon. He asked if I saw him, and I said that I had not.

He said he waited while I loaded them up because he was so sure they would not fit in my vehicle and then he would get them. But, of course, they fit perfectly in my vehicle. So I got them. The irony is that the reason I wanted them was to make a nicer view for him and his wife. I live in the carriage house of an old estate and he lives in the mansion. The property was divided in half sixty years ago and the carriage house expanded into a regular, full-size house. He has a garage, but I don't. I have no utility area and I worry about the side of my house being unattractive to him. You can't really see it much from his place, as I have it covered with wisteria, but I worry about it none-theless. That is why I wanted the trellises—to conceal my storage sheds and utility area. So oddly enough, you could say this was a win-win situation as I am using the trel-lises to make the view more attractive to him. Quite a serendipitous development, yes? —Cherie

* It is not recommended that *Liquid Luck* be listened to while driving or doing anything else that requires alertness, as binaural beat meditations, due to their activating the relaxation response can produce distraction or drowsiness.

Dear Joe, I regularly use Liquid Luck, and I'm very glad about it. Imagine : I sleep much better and I had a funny experience. I put my hands around a spray of flowers, orchids. Especially around one end of one stem of these orchids. And the one flower of this stem mum-mified or fossilized ! It is still in a perfect state for more than six weeks now, while all the other flowers perished normally! —T.K.

Hey Joe, Well here is another Liquid Luck testimonial for you. I went through the Liquid Luck process twice so far for financial luck as far as intentions goes, but not towards any specific financial project. Five years ago, I took a very intense online training on currency trading that is more commonly known as Forex trading. The course was taught by its creator and he didn't take any prisoners. You had to "pay attention" (his favorite phrase to bark) and do your homework assignments on time or he had zero time for you. I am afraid I was not living up to my best as a student because of the distraction from the severe pain from a work injury, depression, and fighting a court battle to stop the workers comp company from discontinuing my payments because they deemed me fit to return to full duty. I wasn't.

I always wanted to get back to retaking the class to redeem myself from my past experience and use it to start earning more income, as I am still disabled from the injury some eight years prior. But each year the price of the training would increase and I was always behind the financial eight ball, so re-taking the class had not happened. I remained on their student mailing list, but had not spoken with them for five years, rebuffing urges to email to say hi.

But a week ago when I got the urge to say hello, for some reason this time I didn't resist and wrote them to say hello, I'm still alive and that "Jim," (the founder who had died from cancer just weeks after my class ended and had left his business to two of his top students) was on a cloud smiling down on how well they have grown the business. And that I wanted to at some point next year retake the class to get back all I have forgotten over the years. That was that . . . or so I thought.

Four days later I received an email welcoming me as a student to the new training starting in one day! These guys gave me free entry into the training that now sells for $2,499.00, fourteen and a quarter times more than when I took it! This wonderful gift came at an inconvenient time, as I am in another training. But this will teach me not to mess around with Liquid Luck if I do not want good stuff to happen for me at "inconvenient" times! LOL. This training is a challenging seven-week time and brain commitment, but I am up for the challenge much more than I was five years ago.

Now I am more psyched than ever to continue priming my experiences with Liquid Luck and I wonder, what's next?

Most of my friends, family, and even my lady would consider getting free access to the Forex training a "coincidence" with playing Liquid Luck. I on the other hand believe that the likelihood of this happening (me obeying the urge to contact the new owners/trainers after five years and them not owing me a thing, and surprising me with a free spot in the current training) without the Liquid Luck process to spark the synchronicity of this happening to be very low.

I will pay close attention in the future to the number of these favorable events occurring by intention. I like doing the Liquid Luck process and will do it up to three times weekly at least until I feel my unconscious firmly "gets" consistently creating the synchronicity of lucky experiences for me is a new top priority. I thought you would like to know, Joe, thanks. Kind regards. —Robert. P.S. Oh, I beat workers comp in court!

Dear Joe, I have actually manifested the Jeep Wrangler I was looking to get, I think Liquid Luck had something to do with it, I was one of the early adopters to the CD. I typically take a day off listening to it in between, but on days when I do an overnight shift (in preparing for the negativity at work) I do three days back to back with some Manifesting with Hemi-Sync and some Liquid Luck. I read your book in December and experienced a delightful romantic interlude shortly after, my belief systems have changed ha-ha!

I thought my power to manifest the new car would be through my hard work, a big savings account and a lot of WILL and FORCE, it had some individual determinism to it, when in fact the money came in from my father as a gift, so I owe some of this manifestation to a collection of things outside my own direct influence. By the way, I am no longer working the gruesome overnight shift, I have a better job now that pays much more. There are some things, maybe negative karma or negative energy, that I can't put my finger on for why I have bad things happen but overall I am enjoying the experience in life. Thanks. —D.R.

Hi Elena, I had listened to Joe's interview with Coast to Coast AM *regarding the release of his Liquid Luck CD and his explanations regarding the concepts. I am pretty (extremely) open-minded and often meditate occasionally utilizing CD's from the Monroe Institute or other binaural beats or alpha and delta range tracks so I thought I'd order myself a copy of Joe's CD. Once the CD arrived I was quick to put it to use but in a more passive sense in that I simply transferred it to my iPod and passively listened to it for a few nights prior to going to sleep. I didn't really feel like I was getting the full benefit of the CD and knew I wasn't really following Joe's instructions and so I decided one night to actively participate whilst listening to the CD.*

I sat myself down in a modified lotus position which I often use for meditative sessions and began focusing on the exact words and instructions Joe was providing. I decided the key to being successful was intense focus and visualisation of the imagery Joe created through his words and the intent behind them. After relaxing my body using various breathing techniques I imagined the various ingredients being poured or whisked into the potion. As it was being constructed I visualised the liquid, the feel of it, the colours, the flask itself and importantly the pouring of my affirmations into the potion. I really felt it was important to reflect upon what Joe was saying and actually realise and believe that I was indeed lucky and had in fact lived a very lucky and blessed life (which I certainly have especially in comparison to so many other people). I poured these realisations into the potions and believed every word and thought I had when I did so.

During the entire experience I kept my thoughts focused purely on Joe's words and his directions and finally I produced a translucent potion which I held in my mind's eye in a small crystal bottle. I drank some of it then and there and imagined it pouring down my throat and spreading throughout my body. Finally I mentally put away the potion for future use. To me the creation of the potion is actually a form of psychic alchemy.

Now at around the same time the new iPad Air was released in Australia. I tried to purchase it but with no luck as every store I went to in Perth was sold out. I went to purchase it online via the Apple store but after all the extra's and insurances I was looking at spending over $2,000. When I had virtually given up hope of purchasing one in the immediate future and for a reasonable price, I was alerted to a raffle our firm had just initiated where the prize was exactly what I was after—a 32GB iPad Air!

Our marketing manager asked if I'd like a ticket and I said I would take 3 for $20. Just before I handed over my $20 I retrieved my liquid luck potion and took a deep swig of it whilst reciting in my mind a winning mantra and an affirmation of my own luck and inherent luck and good fortune in life. I took my tickets and exchanged my money and, as I did so, I just knew I would win. It wasn't wishful thinking. This was different in that somehow I just knew.

The draw wasn't for a couple more weeks and various people bought their tickets and there was plenty of office banter regarding the prize. I didn't engage in it and wasn't anxious about the outcome as I just knew the outcome would be in my favour. I wasn't arrogant in my thoughts but peaceful and content in the knowledge I had. The night of the draw was a charity quiz night and I wasn't able to attend. I had actually forgotten about it until later on that night when I thought to myself, "I bet I get a call tonight telling me I won." Later that night I was taking a shower and sure enough my mobile started to ring and I knew instantly it was one of my friends from work telling me I had won the iPad. In fact my mobile rang several times and chimed with a few messages as multiple people left various messages telling me I'd won the iPad Air. I didn't rush to answer any of them at the time. I just knew and was thankful to the universe for my good fortune.

I truly believe that properly performing and visualising the instructions that Joe provided on the Liquid Luck CD provided me with the knowledge to create a potent potion that literally increased my luck from a chance into a certainty. I felt absolutely certain I would win. There was no doubt and that in itself is odd as usually everyone is affected by 'negative speak' at some point but this time my belief was unwavering. It felt more like actual knowledge of success rather than a belief or a hope. So thank you Joe! I use my iPad Air everyday and truly feel luckier as a result! Kind regards. —Drew

Hi Joe, this happened on the weekend before I left for my Inner Vegas Adventure. I sell my paintings for a living on Jackson Square in New Orleans. I had a slew of bills to pay before I left and was counting on the weekend before leaving to make $2,000. I made half of it on Saturday and was counting on Sunday for the rest. I did the Liquid Luck meditation before I went to bed on Saturday night. I woke up Sunday morning to all day rain. Talk about a disappointment. A couple of hours later I received a phone call from a woman who wanted a painting. I needed another $1,000 before I left. The painting was $1,200. She told me that her husband said that she could buy it if it was under a thousand so I let her have it for $999. Thanks Joe. —Barbara

I'm working on a Liquid Luck testimonial, I've got some incredible comments for you regarding the new ideas that have come to me while listening to Liquid Luck. My business that had been fairly stagnant took off with hundreds of new orders. I solved a difficult circuit design problem and have come up with a fantastic new design for a new replacement product. This was also inspired during listening to Liquid Luck! Cheers. —A.S.

Thank you! Thank you! Thank you! Thank you for what you both do, what you've created in this program, and thank you for making your products so accessible! I'm sure I will be spreading this program as love to my friends and family, and I hope they benefit as I have through my mom! Money has little to do with why I love this meditation, feeling so bright, light, and blessed everyday is incredible and I feel contagious! Blessings to you and yours. —C.P.

Amazing! Since using Liquid Luck I have won eight days in a row at roulette. I just visualize taking a drink of Liquid Luck while I am at the roulette table and the win happens very quickly. —R.S.

I have some interesting things to report about using your Liquid Luck. I could not help but fall very deeply asleep when listening to Liquid Luck the first couple times. I was so grateful for this because I often have sleep stressors like trouble sleeping, vivid nightmares, and thoughts of problems I have trouble solving. I wake up hitting myself in the head because I am sure I have forgotten something important. Over and over. In contrast with Liquid Luck I slept deeply.

So while I was in Vegas last week, I was listening while running on the Strip early morning, which I love to do. It's sort of trance like for me. I loved it and actually got to hear the meditation. One night I was down about a hundred from blackjack and we went to play craps. Bought in for a hundred dollars and went on a monster roll, I guess at least twenty minutes, and had a long row of chips ahead of me. That was so fun! We did have a wonderful time. I was a little disappointed about not doing better at the tables with Liquid Luck, except for that awesome craps roll, but I feel like it manifested in other ways, like really connecting with my parents and my brother and just getting to spend stress-free time with them . . . happy, relaxed moments with my dad are highly valuable to me. Thanks for the great meditation. When I got home, it turns out that my nine-year-old's puppy had been hit by a car while I was gone. He had not one injury and is totally fine. All the best. —Melanie

---

Dear Joe, I have reviewed your book on Amazon and gave it five stars, my pleasure. I have just started some of the manifestation meditations with your CDs in the last week. Today my daughter found an expensive ruby and gold ring that I bought for my wife seven or eight years ago. It had been lost for at least four years, maybe five. My wife and I had given it up for gone a long time ago. She found it buried in the glove compartment of my wife's old car. When I saw the ring I immediately thought of Inner Vegas and Liquid Luck. Maybe it is just a coincidence . . . or maybe not, and that is certainly far more interesting. —Michel

---

Joe, got the disks on Friday. Listened during a catnap. Next day an unexpected check for $3,000.00 was delivered. —Alan

---

Dear Dr. Gallenberger, It is not often that I write to a manufacturer of a product that I've purchased. As a scientist, engineer, and product designer, I avoid any products that have no scientific merit. In the case of your revolutionary product Liquid Luck, I was so dramatically impressed with the results that I felt compelled to let you know about my experience with your amazing product.

As mentioned above, my current job description is that of a product designer, and I often find inspiration difficult to come by. Days or weeks go by without a glimmer of a new product in my mind—that is, until I was exposed to Liquid Luck! Listening to this Compact Disc with headphones right before I retire for the evening, Liquid Luck enables me to "quiet" my busy mind and releases powers in my imagination. I have overcome my "block" and am working on an innovative series of products that I attribute to my new-found inspiration.

A meditative theme, with relaxing ambient sounds, takes you away from the daily grind; Dr. Gallenberger's

verbal instructions instills your subconscious mind with new thoughts that will remove your mundane world and instead replace it with a world of wonder, peace, and energy. I heartily recommend using Liquid Luck on a daily basis, whether you're a designer or just someone who is seeking more inner peace. Sincerely. —Albert Von Schweikert, Chief Design Engineer

---

Joe's note: Albert designs amazing stereo speakers. He and I share a deep love of music. We have developed a friendship over the years and I have a pair of his speakers. He invents innovative products from very affordable to stratospheric in price and quality and all very musical. Recently he called me, excited to share that he had been blocked for eighteen months in attempts to design a state-of-the-art half a million dollar speaker system, and with Liquid Luck has able to run through complex mathematical options in his imagination and discover the solution he was seeking. The speakers are now in production.

Chapter 11

BINAURAL BEAT MEDITATION

I wanted to let you know some of the results I have produced from listening to the CD Liquid Luck. First let me say the CD is so calming. My body feels calm and my mind feels alert. I love it. I use the information on Liquid Luck to tap into my intuition better. For example, the other day I was out running errands and needed to stop for gas. While at the gas station I thought about the pattern I had learned through Liquid Luck and used it. I got the idea to buy some scratch-off lottery tickets for my husband as a surprise. So I bought him five $1 scratch off tickets. When he scratched them off, he had won $21. A great bit of fun. Thank you, Dr. Joe. —Ann

I promised in the introduction of this book to go into more detail about binaural beat technology. In this chapter I will discuss what it is and how it can help with meditation. We will look specifically at how it is used in Liquid Luck to facilitate rapid and deep shifts in consciousness, allowing for new creativity and energy to be applied to the creation of luck and abundance. The most researched variant of binaural beat technology is called Hemi-Sync®, so we will examine this quite carefully.

A large variety of methods of contemplation and meditation from various religious systems are very effective at altering consciousness and have great value. But most of them require years of study and practice to attain consistency and proficiency. Examples of these include centering prayer, chanting, yoga, and chi-gong. They may require the adoption of a particular set of religious or philosophical beliefs and some have been adapted for Western use.

There are quite a few meditation methods developed in the past fifty years that use the assistance of sound and/or light technologies that aide in the process of altering consciousness. Most of these are free of the need to adopt any particular beliefs for them to be effective. While they may work well according to self-reports, few have been studied in any scientific way.

The system that I think has the best research behind it and is most effective for most people is binaural beat technology. And the most studied binaural beat technology in terms of research and application over the last few decades is the Hemi-Sync system designed by Robert Monroe. I must state that this whole field is a vast and somewhat uncharted area and there may indeed be as good or better technologies out there, but that this Hemi-Sync binaural beat system is the one I am most familiar with. I have used it myself and seen thousands of others use it over a period of thirty years. Given this, Hemi-Sync will be our reference point for discussing how binaural beat technology works and is helpful to those exploring the manifestation path.

I have been a trainer of residential programs at Monroe Institute in Virginia for about twenty-three years, and a participant in their programs for a few years longer. I travel there about ten times a year, each time to train one of their week-long programs. Perhaps Bob Monroe's most brilliant invention was his Hemi-Sync system. Hemi-Sync stands for the term hemispheric synchronization, which refers to synchronizing the two hemispheres of the brain. In this system, stereo headphones are employed to provide each ear with a slightly different steady tone. This causes what is termed a binaural beat, which is heard as a warbling tone in the center of the head. This tone does not really exist outside the brain. Rather it is created by the brain when exposed to two slightly different tones, one in each ear.

One interesting thing is that when this binaural beat happens, the person's brain waves tend to synchronize between the right and left hemispheres of the brain. This facilitates more communication between the brain hemispheres, resulting in a more whole brain focused-learning state, compared to our usual state of consciousness. In some ways it is like helping our brain power move from a scattered radiation similar to a light bulb, to focusing it more like a laser.

Sound waves are measured in cycles per second. Human beings can usually hear sounds in the range of twenty cycles per second to twenty thousand cycles per second. Our brain waves can also be measured in cycles per second and usually span from a very slow one cycle per second to a fairly rapid fifty cycles per second or higher. In addition to synchronizing the hemispheres, binaural beats tend to move the brain-wave patterns to the speed of the difference between the two tones (one in each ear). So if the difference between the two tones is four cycles per second, the brain tends to begin to also go into a four-cycle-per-second rhythm. If another difference is presented over the headphones such as ten cycles per second, then the brain tends to go into a ten-cycle-per-second pattern.

The binaural beat effect was discovered in 1839 by Heinrich Wilhelm Dove, but studied only occasionally until over one hundred years later when Gerald Oster revived interest in the subject with new research[13]. The effects of binaural beats on consciousness were then examined by physicist Thomas Warren Campbell and electrical engineer Dennis Mennerich. They worked under the direction of Robert Monroe. Mr. Monroe then added facilitating sound effects and verbal guidance to the binaural beats and found this effective for altering consciousness in directions desired. He called this mix of all three components (beat, sound effects, and verbal guidance) Hemi-Sync. He received an original patent in 1975 for this Hemi-Sync mixture and its ability to enhance consciousness.

We know that different cycles per second in brain-wave patterns tend to correlate with the different states of consciousness. For example, the one to four cycles per second pattern is called the delta range and tends to be present when we are deeply asleep. Many other brain-wave patterns have been identified such as four to seven cycles, called the theta range, which is often present in deep meditative states. Cycles of seven to fourteen are called the alpha range and are present in lighter meditation states and daydreaming, and fourteen to twenty-five cycles, called the beta range, occur during awake states. There is a state called gamma that involves brain wave frequencies of twenty-five to fifty cycles per second. Gamma states are particularly significant to our discussion in that they seem to be associated with psychic phenomena such as energy healing and PK. There are higher brain waves called epsilon, which at this time have just begun to attract researchers' attention.

One can also combine different binaural beat patterns together at the same time, such as delta and beta patterns. Such

---

13 Auditory Beats in the Brain by Gerald Oster's (*Scientific American*, 1973).

a pattern can result in a state where the body is simultaneously deeply asleep (delta) and the mind still awake and aware (beta). In this state, many people are surprised to be awake, yet hearing themselves snore! Such a state is excellent for very deep relaxation, pain control, accelerated healing, and receiving intuition.

Many states of consciousness have been mapped, each having particular qualities and uses to it. In the Monroe system different patterns of binaural beats and their most common resulting patterns of consciousness are called "Focus levels." These focus levels are then designated by numbers. In the Monroe system, Focus One is ordinary awake consciousness. Focus Three relates to the increased synchronization of brain hemispheres or whole brain activation. Focus Ten is the body-asleep-mind-awake state already mentioned. Focus Twelve is called a state of expanded awareness and an activation of the ability to perceive information beyond what is usually available through the physical senses. Focus Twelve can be thought of as activating our sixth sense or our psychic senses. By the time a person's brain waves have shifted from Focus One, our usual consciousness, to Focus Twelve, there are profound differences in how we process information and get answers to questions. This can come in very handy for unleashing creative thought processes such as my engineer friend used to solve problems and have inspiration for inventions. Often in Focus Twelve states solutions pop up that would have seemed just too simple from the perspective of Focus One everyday consciousness and therefore would never have arisen for consideration.

Binaural beat technology delivered through headphones is a terrific tool for changing consciousness in many ways, and are helpful in the PK, energy healing, and the manifestation process.

It allows a rapid, dogma-free training, so that a person can manage their emotional and mental states with much greater control. At its most basic, we can use this technology to simply relax and move into the present moment. We have found this to be very useful in abundance creation because it allows us to let go of fear and limiting thinking and soften the ego-driven monkey mind's grip on our consciousness.

Some binaural beat patterns are designed to facilitate access to even deeper levels of consciousness. These levels facilitate a transcending of the usual limits of time-space perception both to think more creatively and to open up one's potential to be in touch with non-physical energies and dimensions. Here intuition, guidance, and wisdom are more accessible. These higher states of awareness come in handy with PK and energy healing because they seem to utilize energies that transcend the usual rules of time-space. Finally, by helping to quiet left-brain consciousness, binaural beat technologies can help us become more aware of our own heart consciousness or heart energy. We have shown that the power of love is the greatest of all powers that can help us with manifesting our dreams.

Binaural beat exercises are efficient and practical. They are mostly about a half-hour long and can be easily used from a compact disc or loaded onto portable electronic devices such as iPods, Android systems, and iPhones and be carried around conveniently. All you need to do is to relax in a chair or bed, put on the headphones and listen. There is no need to spend years studying some esoteric system. The headphone part may be significant. The hemispheric synchronization under binaural beat stimulation has been proven to occur compared to placebo in double blind studies. However, a study using air-conduction tubes to deliver the sound, rather than headphones, failed to produce the synchronization, suggesting that perhaps the electromagnetic stimulation of the headphones may lead to a stronger effect, rather than just an acoustic presentation such as hearing the sound over speakers.

In the Liquid Luck meditation the combination of changing binaural beats, plus sounds that facilitate movements in consciousness and verbal guidance all combine to take the listener on a journey of expanded awareness. At the beginning of the exercise the three factors combine to help one rapidly relax. Next there is guidance to off-load any distractions and to have concerns put aside and transformed into new positive energy patterns. This is very useful for quieting any fear or limiting beliefs. The listener is then guided to begin raising their consciousness and energy with the help of changing binaural beats and sound effects. Once in a high energy open-hearted state, there is gentle verbal guidance to create the vial of Liquid Luck. Here is where the energies of happiness, gratitude, abundance, love, praise, and good fortune are added. The exercise includes how this container of Liquid Luck can be utilized with the following words:

When you want to use your potion all you need do is imagine your container filled with the swirling liquid, hold it between your fingers . . . see it sparkle with the energies of happiness, gratitude, abundance, compassion, love, praise, and good fortune . . . Then, take a drink . . . and all parts of your being, from your conscious mind, your unconscious, your energy body, your inner child wisdom, through your highest self, and down to the quantum energy in every cell will align and harmonize to create a wonderfully lucky day for you where good fortune abounds and you reach your goals easily and effortlessly. The more often you use your Liquid Luck the more powerful and effective it will become.

As you can see, Liquid luck is designed so that once the potion is formed it can be used without the need the take the time to go through the full meditation again. This way it can be employed on-the-fly in real life, for example before an important meeting, right before buying a lotto ticket, or at the beginning of a day where you are actively working on manifesting something highly valuable to you. Given this, I was initially surprised at how many people reported listening to the exercise itself nearly every day because they found that doing so put them in such a great mood where creativity, confidence, and good feeling flowed. Upon reflection, this made perfect sense given the powerful effect of the binaural beat technology and the emphasis on activating the high energies from happiness to love during the meditation.

The Liquid Luck exercise ends by guiding the listener gently back down into normal waking consciousness with the help for the binaural beats changing back to those beats that support a relaxed but awake and alert state. This is done in a way that accents the powerful effect of trusting and letting go that was covered in the Chapter entitled "Synchronicity, Serendipity, Timing, and Trust."

Now simply let go, releasing your pattern out to the farthest reaches of your awareness. Release your pattern and trust the universe to create this pattern for you and with you . . . Just let go and relax. You can now make space and energy available for your new creation to enter your life by simply letting go.

Resting now . . . calm, confident, and comfortable and open to receiving all good, opening to the new positive energies and patterns that will come into your life.

Now, it is time to return to normal waking consciousness. Please gently begin to bring your awareness fully back into your body as you listen to this affirmation . . . "I enjoy new energy by grounding. I allow my spirit's energy and light to fill my body. I am nurtured by the sacred energies of the earth, so that I am fully spirit and flesh at the same time and I am fully present to each sacred moment."

You will remember and integrate all you have experienced for your great benefit.

So now you understand where much of the magic in Liquid Luck comes from. It is in this combination of the highest energies generated and focused in a particular way to facilitate creation of our dreams. It is able to be so rapid and powerful because of the exceptional utility of binaural beat meditation to aid this process.

Chapter 12

TOOLS FOR MASTERING
MANIFESTATION

Hey Joe, I noticed that the results that come from raising energy don't hap-
pen right away or in the same day. I found that I was not being given business
at this difficult gym where I am a personal trainer. I did the Liquid Luck
meditation. Then I got a call from someone who is in another very busy gym,
it was a day or two after doing Liquid Luck, and she called me saying how
well she was doing and invited me over. They have a lot of volume to keep up
with, and now I'm in the process of transferring over. In time I'll be able to
practice more of my manifesting skills to do the SyncCreation program and
the workshop. Best regards. —Damian

If one decides to engage in a thorough study of PK, energy healing, and the manifestation process, to it make it a yoga or pathway that they want to deeply understand and to become proficient at no matter what the circumstance, then more extensive tools become necessary. Folks who have taken the time to read this book this far may be in that camp. Perhaps you have had some success with the Liquid Luck meditation or other forms of manifestation, but there are still areas in your life that seem limited or lagging behind. It is here that these additional tools may help. And even if instead you feel totally negative, powerless, and blocked and suspect that the concepts presented here are either overly optimistic or do not apply to you and your situation, these additional tools to address fear and limits may help.

This book already contains a wealth of tools that are now at your disposal. They represent my best thinking on what are the basics to master if you become a serious student of manifestation. Cultivating and nourishing the energies of happiness, gratitude, abundance, compassion, praise, and love, and doing so in a grounded fashion can be nothing but positive and is often profoundly healing and empowering on the path. These energies themselves will often quiet or slay many heads of the fear dragon.

In case you want or need to go further, I would like to present a buffet of other tools in no particular order. At a buffet you need not eat everything, but often cruise along finding the foods that call to you at the moment. Similarly here, a great approach is to just cruise through these offerings and note the tools that call to you as most appropriate for your next step along your path. Then take action and try that particular offering as the instrument of growth for you. You are seeking to dramatically increase your self-awareness and explore more deeply through understanding and experience that which interests you here, be it PK, energy healing, manifestation, or all of these skills. Self-awareness is essential to discover your true nature as a miracle creator, and to find where you might be blocked. Many of these tools are free, and some cost varying amounts of time and money. Before starting to assess these tools affirm that you are worth the time and investment, and that you are going to find the right approach that greatly benefits you and those around you.

First off, let nothing stop you! Let everything become a source of learning. If you blow it occasionally like I and everybody else I know does, and get into a fight, frustration, or funk, allow it to be a teaching moment, and avoid derailing yourself by going into self-criticism, victim-consciousness, or judgment. This journey is a marathon, not a sprint, so take time to just rest and "veg out." Keeping a record of your experiences and even significant dreams in a journal can be very helpful to track progress and gain insight.

There is of course many books on these subjects. There is a section called Suggested Readings at the end of this book mentioning some books that I and others have found central to their journeys. My own book *Inner Vegas: Creating Miracles, Abundance, and Health* is about much more than Vegas, and covers much about psychokinesis, energy healing, and transcending personal dragons.

Another great source of information now is through websites which contain everything from sites on which to take part in PK and intuition experiments, to sites such as YouTube where many videos are available on these topics. I have had people report seeing one of the videos there on spoon-bending and then immediately being able to duplicate the PK and bend a spoon at home. Many of the radio shows that I have done in the past year are on the web, as well as many famous inspirational speakers in the self-empowerment and manifestation areas. An excellent way to find them is to enter a term such as psychokinesis or energy healing and see what pops up. My website,[14] SyncCreation.com, has lots of free tips and articles on the topics that we have been exploring.

---

14 http://synccreation.com/previous-articles/

A wonderful way to learn in depth is to ask to be the apprentice of someone who demonstrates the skill set that you would like to learn. Many highly successful business people realize the value of and enjoy helping others learn what they do and know. An excellent way to learn energy healing is to work with a proficient healer, perhaps first as a client and then as an apprentice. There are many schools of healing and often the more established and successful have certification programs which can help you find someone and perhaps offer you a path of study if this area interests you.

Psychotherapy, counseling, and coaching all can provide great benefits in terms of self-awareness, support, and empowerment to change. Since this involves an extensive commitment and is so private and personal, it is helpful to carefully interview the possible candidate for this role in your life. Here, referrals by someone you trust can help identify possible mentors. Part of the interview process would be to ask about theoretical orientation, their knowledge of the areas we have been discussing, and if their approach is present-oriented, practical, and empowering. For example, for psychotherapy I would select a therapist who focuses on the present and helps me identify and utilize my strengths. And I would ask, "Have you heard of positive psychology? What does it mean to you? How do you generally view your client and go about empowering them?"

Working with someone can seem a strange thing to do if you never have done it before and may rub against beliefs, such as the belief that you are showing weakness because you are supposed to be able to handle things by yourself. But many of the most successful people in their fields use mentors, counselors, and coaches and at times even support groups because they want to continue to improve on their excellence. I would suspect that even Tiger Woods uses a golf coach!

There are many high-quality seminars offered on these topics. Besides the content, a highly valuable contribution to your path can be the other people you meet at such an event. They can confirm that you are not crazy to be focusing on these things, offer guidance and support, and even become life-long friends. It can be very lonely to explore these topics if your family and current friends do not share your interests. There are seminars on energy healing methods, and ones on creating the reality that you desire, as well as seminars that explore specific types of abundance creation such as investing in real estate, or starting a small business. Some of these are filled with hype and come-ons, so be sure to get references from people who have actually attended.

The best place that I have found to deeply explore your own consciousness is The Monroe Institute[15] (TMI), mentioned in this book and more extensively in *Inner Vegas*. I have been a participant and trainer there for almost thirty years. It is located in a beautiful rural setting, has the amazing brainwave technology, Hemi-Sync to deepen meditation quickly, is free of dogma, attracts a worldwide group of intelligent and caring explorers, and has highly interesting experiential programs and very well trained facilitators. As mentioned, I developed TMI's MC² program (Manifestation and Creation Squared) which specifically deals with these areas of PK, energy healing, and manifestation. MC² is a TMI graduate program, requiring their Gateway program as a pre-requisite.

---

15 MonroeInstitute.org

However I occasionally offer SyncCreation[16] workshops for people who have not attended Gateway. Monroe Institute has weekend programs using the same technology that explore consciousness in many communities around the world. The schedule of these activities is on their website. They also have Local Chapter Networks in many places in the USA and in other countries, where people gather to experience consciousness explorations and fellowship together with other folks in their community, often on a monthly basis.

I offer the Inner Vegas Adventure[17] workshops in Las Vegas, which focus on these three areas, using the casino as the classroom for quick and clear feedback. In the seventy workshops done so far I feel we have seen PK demonstrated in each one to varying degrees, as well as had significant healing and insights on the part of the participants. I cannot guarantee that you will win back your tuition, but you just might!

I also offer a home study course on these topics, called *SyncCreation: A Course in Manifestation*[18] that well over a thousand people have used and rated very highly. My website contains much more information than is presented here, including a survey of the results that people have experienced. SyncCreation comes with a dozen custom Hemi-Sync meditation exercises, an extensive hundred-page book containing many experiential exercises on the topics we have covered including PK metal bending, seed growing, light bulb lighting, and healing self and others, as feedback tools to measure progress and to learn about creation with your energy

---

16 http://synccreation.com/synccreation-workshop/
17 http://synccreation.com/inner-vegas/
18 http://synccreation.com/the-course/

and thought. There are also powerful exercises for grounding and clearing blocks of fear and limits. Two hours of personal coaching come with the course.

Besides *Liquid Luck* I also offer other individual downloads and CD exercises[19]. These include: *Manifesting with Hemi-Sync* which has two exercises for visualizing what you would like to create. *Partner's Meditation*, designed to elevate your energy in all your important relationships, past or present, which is very helpful in raising and maintaining your energy for manifestation. And my newest CD/download called *Abundance Waterfall*, which is designed to have you appreciate and then increase abundance in all areas of your life.

So there is much help out there. Get the assistance you need, keep the faith (in yourself and the world) and enjoy this amazing journey we call life!

---

19 http://synccreation.com/hemi-sync/

Chapter 13

SUMMARY

I am an experienced realtor who hates hosting open houses! I was at one this week, bored out of my mind, because no one was coming to see the $650,000 property. Then I remembered listening to Liquid Luck a few days before. I took a drink of Liquid Luck and within twenty minutes a couple came by and loved the house. They did not have their checkbook with them. I just surrendered to what would be best for all concerned and they bought the house within three days! —A.H.

We have covered a lot of ground in this book. In understanding manifestation, it is important to remember that it is really a natural process. As we have dissected the creation process into its significant parts, there is a danger that we have made something that is our birthright seem so complicated as to be intimidating. We could look in such detail at many normal processes that we carry on daily without a thought, such as breathing or digestion, and experience the same type of wonder at their complexity. But we would not allow that wonder to keep us from breathing!

This also occurs with many learned skills. When we first break down piano playing into reading music, learning all the notes, and the notations concerning length and timing of those notes, and the positions of the hands, etc., it can seem cumbersome and overwhelming. When we learn a particular dance step, we first must understand where to put our feet, how to hold our partner, and how the sequence of movements proceeds. It is the same here. Yes, in manifestation many factors interact with each other, but they do so in a rhythm that with practice soon becomes very natural.

We see that happiness is important to life satisfaction and health and that it enhances and is helped by grounding, which is being fully present in the here and now. They become a positive feedback loop for each other. The happier we are, the more grounded we tend to become and the more grounded we are, the happier we will tend to be. As both increase our manifestation, effectiveness increases. As more of our dreams are created, we become even more grounded and happy because it is more fun and satisfying to be here!

We have shown that practicing gratitude for the blessings we already possess fosters happiness. The better we are at manifesting, the more opportunities we have to feel grateful. Next, we added feeling abundant to the mix because under the principle of "Like Attracts Like," if we feel lacking in an area we will tend to manifest more lack, and if we feel abundant, we will tend to produce more abundance.

With these basics in place, we can greatly amplify our abundance creation by connecting with sources outside of our main concern with ourselves. The first way we do this is to cultivate more compassion. This serves to connect us with others and motivates us to create abundance and happiness for many besides ourselves. Thus, the universe is tempted to help us more actively, given that our efforts will now have even farther-reaching positive impact. As we practice compassion, it also helps us become more compassionate toward ourselves, which can help release the many ways we might block goodness from coming to ourselves, such as guilt and self-criticism.

We then add love to the mix, which even more deeply connects us to others, to the world and to spirit, and further opens the tremendous power of our hearts. With love we will have the courage to go forward into the unknown of change. With love we can be trusted to stay out of greed and ego, and use the wisdom of the heart to select what we create for the benefit of all. With love we link to all consciousness in the universe and have seen that consciousness and love may be the essential underpinning of the entire time/space universe and beyond.

Next we add praise as a natural outpouring in celebration of the energies we are engaging. This praise aligns us with the highest and finest energies of the universe, joining our song with the song of all of creation and the angels, if you will. The power of praise assures that our path will be true to the design of the universe for best purpose and will empower our manifestation even further.

Finally, at the moment that we are likely to already be feeling fortunate from our resonance with all the energies mentioned so far, we add the energy of luck to our energy mix. The addition of a lucky feeling allows synchronicity and serendipity to come into play more strongly and makes it easier to have trust and sense the correct timing to take action towards our creation. And feeling lucky we have the confidence to take a chance and create something new.

Now with all the notes learned, we can play the music and dance the dance of creating such good in our lives that it can appear miraculous. At first we may be self-conscious and stumble a bit and that is perfectly natural and okay. Remember that each present moment is freely given and within it we can choose differently.

I would like to tell a true story that illustrates the way self-consciousness can play out in hampering our energy. From a very young age I was at home on ice skates. All my friends and I looked forward to when the local pond would freeze. It was a rare treat, in that some winters in New Jersey it never froze solid enough to skate. I played a bit of informal ice hockey but really liked figure skating and if I do say so myself, was smooth in my moves. What I know for certain is that I had tremendous fun, going forward at great speed, executing turns, small jumps and skating backwards, losing track of time until my feet were numb.

I felt the same joy and competence with roller skates at the roller rink and local streets. In fact perhaps the first contest that I won (manifested) was coloring in a drawing of Huey, Dewey, and Louie Duck for a national contest and winning a pair of really fancy roller skates when I was about eight years old.

I want to contrast this with the first time I went to a dance. Here I was very concerned with looking cool and doing it right because this is how you captured a girl's (hopefully favorable) attention. A girl's attention was one of the most hoped for and feared experiences that a young adolescent boy could dream of. I gave dancing a shot. I felt self-conscious and uneasy, constantly monitoring my movements and scanning around to see if anyone was watching. I felt I was moving "like a chicken with its head cut off," felt very embarrassed and terminated the experience as fast as I could. What is up here? Dancing on a wooden floor in shoes has got to be easier than dancing on skates—unless you are self-conscious! So, as you do your manifestation work, let go judging yourself and of worrying what anybody else thinks! Some will say you are crazy, or that any good results are coincidence. Some might be envious. Some might even say that you are in league with the devil if you have success.

As with learning to play an instrument or to dance, it is perfectly appropriate to start with smaller, simpler steps. It may be too much (or maybe not) to attempt to move from feeling much scarcity in your life, directly to winning a hundred-million-dollar lottery. But manifesting a sweet parking space or a $100 win on a scratch ticket might be easier for many reasons. You have an easier time believing that it is possible and that you are worth it, and that it will not rock your world too dramatically.

We have seen that there are simple CD's and many books including the ones on the recommended reading list in this book that can help ignite your manifestation ability. My hope is that you use this book, *Liquid Luck*, as a handy handbook, that you go back to often to refresh your understanding and enthusiasm for abundance creation. And if you want to go more deeply in this journey there are workshops and home study courses that can help you.

The main thing that can get in the way is fear. It can cloud any part of the process, so it is important to identify, manage, and melt fear. The self-consciousness mentioned above is but one example of fear. If it is helpful to you, you can view fear as a multi-headed dragon guarding your treasured goals. And know that in the end, it is a dragon of your own creation and is no match for you, as you are a powerful embodied spirit designed to be a creator of all good. The dragon only has the amount of power that you give it. Remember your affirmations: "I am free of all Limits, I am of great Light."; "I am of great Love."; and, "I accept myself as most honored guest in my own heart." Then simply sing the dragon to sleep with your own high heart energy which is love, and move onward and upward.

Once you have learned the notes or the steps, playing an instrument or dancing becomes easier and can be great fun and a unique way to express who you are. In the same manner, learning to consistently create abundance in your life becomes easier, then great fun and a wonderful way to express the uniqueness that is you. You will put your very own spin on it as you express your heart's desires into reality. It will benefit you, and the world will benefit as you live a happy and abundant life! Thank you so much for reading this book. I hope it helps bring every blessing to you and your community. Good Luck!

RECOMMENDED WEBSITES

www.Heartmath.org
The Institute of Heart Math

www.Hemi-Sync.com
Monroe Products Hemi-Sync
exercises by download and on CD

www.icrl.org
International Consciousness Research Laboratories,
successors to Princeton Engineering Anomalous Research lab
(PEAR)

www.MonroeInstitue.org
The Monroe Institute's residential programs and research
activities. Also carries Hemi-Sync and other CDs.

www.noetic.org
The Institute for Noetic Sciences (IONS)

www.Psyleron.com
Products that explore psychokinesis

www.scientificexploration.org
The Society for Scientific Exploration

www.SyncCreation.com
The author Joe Gallenberger's website for information about his products and services including the SyncCreation Home study course, SyncCreation workshops, the Inner Vegas Adventure workshops, and CD/Downloads of Liquid Luck, Abundance Waterfall, Partner's Meditation, and Manifesting with Hemi-Sync.

Appendix 2

RECOMMENDED READINGS

These books are useful in expanding one's understanding of the manifestation process and understanding the nature of reality. I have given a short description of what each book is about. Pick a few that you are called to intuitively. I hope you enjoy them as much as I have.

Peter L. Bernstein, *Against the Gods: The Remarkable Story of Risk* (New York, NY: John Wiley & Sons, 1996). Very useful book to understand risk, and its psychological aspects better.

Gregg Braden, Ph.D., *Deep Truth: Igniting the Memory of Our Origin, History, Destiny, and Fate* (Carlsbad, CA: Hay House, 2011). Challenges conventional assumptions about the history of human culture.

Robert Bruce, *Astral Dynamics: A New Approach to Out of Body Experiences* (Charlottesville, VA: Hampton Roads Publishing Company, 1999). Has good energy exercises.

Julia Cameron, *The Artist's Way: A Spiritual Path to Higher Creativity* (New York, NY: Penguin Putnam, 1991). Excellent creativity exercises.

Chris Carter, *Science and Psychic Phenomena: The Fall of the House of Skeptics* (Rochester, VT: Inner Traditions, 2007). Describes overview of what has been proven in the PK and PSI areas and why there is so much resistance to the findings and from whom.

Doc Childre and Howard Martin, *The Heartmath Solution* (New York, NY: Harper Collins, 1999). Practical guide on how to harness your own heart energy for improved health and consciousness.

Paulo Coelho, *The Alchemist* (San Francisco, CA: HarperCollins Publishers Inc., 1994). A simple allegory about finding and following your dream to full actualization, that I think well describes some of the sacred rhythms within this adventure.

Course in Miracles, A (Tiburon, CA: Foundation for Inner Peace, 1985). A spiritual system that emphasizes inner work from a nontraditional Christian perspective.

Paul Dong, Thomas Rafill, and Karen Kramer Ph.D., *China's Super Psychics* (Cambridge, MA: Marlowe & Company, 1997). Describes research and results from China's extensive program for developing psychics.

Joseph Gallenberger , Ph.D., *Inner Vegas: Creating Miracles, Abundance, and Health* (Faber, VA: Rainbow Ridge Books, 2012). Describes author's journey learning about psychokinesis, energy healing, and abundance.

Malcolm Gladwell, *Blink: The Power of Thinking without Thinking* (New York, NY: Back Bay Books, 2007). Explores how small actions can create rapid and profound change.

Malcolm Gladwell, *Outliers: The Story of Success* (New York, NY: Little, Brown and Company, 2008). Talks about factors contributing to success.

John Hasted, *The Metal-Benders* (London, UK: Routledge & Kegan Paul Ltd., 1981). Explores metal bending from a scientific point of view.

Pamela Rae Heath M.D., Psy.D., *The PK Zone: A Cross-cultural Review of Psychokinesis (PK)* (New York, NY: iUniverse, Inc., 2003). Well documented overview of the psychokinesis literature.

Gay Hendricks and Kate Ludeman, *The Corporate Mystic : A Guidebook for Visionaries with Their Feet on the Ground* (New York, NY: Bantam Books, 1996). Discusses the importance of integrity to manifestation individually and in business.

Ester and Jerry Hicks, *The Law of Attraction: The Basic Teachings of Abraham* (Carlsbad, CA: Hay House, 2006). Explores the seminal idea that like attracts like.

Three Initiates, *The Kybalion* (New York, NY: Tarcher/Penguin, 2008). Presents manifestation wisdom from the Middle Egyptian period.

Bruce Lipton, *The Biology of Belief: Unleashing the Power of Consciousness, Matter and Miracles* (Santa Rosa, CA: Mountain of Love/Elite Books, 2005). An excellent presentation of the newest in biological thought that challenges some of the most deeply held limiting beliefs such as "survival of the fittest."

Jim Loehr and Tony Schwartz, *The Power of Full Engagement: Managing Energy Not Time is the Key to High Performance and Personal Renewal* (New York, NY: Free Press, 2005). Talks about managing energy, not time, as the key to enhanced success.

Richard Madaus, *Think Logically, Live Intuitively: Seeking the Balance* (Charlottesville, VA: Hampton Roads Publishing Company, 2005). Explores the roles of intuition and logic in creating a good life.

Caroline Myss, *Energy Anatomy: The Science of Personal Power, Spirituality and Health (CDs)* (Louisville, CO: Sounds True, Inc., 2001). Excellent series of CD's that explain the body's energy systems and how to work with them for emotional and physical healing.

Dean Radin, Ph.D., *The Conscious Universe: The Scientific Truth of Psychic Phenomena* (San Francisco, CA: Harper-Collins Publishers Inc., 1997). A good overview of the data behind PK and other psychic functioning.

Martin Seligman, *Authentic Happiness: Using the New Positive Psychology to Realize Your Potential for Lasting Fulfillment* (New

York, NY: Free Press, 2002). Excellent summary of findings on the importance of happiness and how to become happier.

David Spangler, *Everyday Miracles: The Inner Art of Manifestation* (New York, NY: Bantam Books, 1996). Talks of the co-creation process.

Jill Bolte Taylor, Ph.D., *My Stroke of Insight: A Brain Scientists personal Journey* (New York, NY: Viking, 2008). Talks about left and right brain consciousness from the perspective of a neuroscientist who suffered a stroke.

Eckhart Tolle, *The Power of Now: A Guide to Spiritual Enlightenment* (Navato, CA: New World Library, 2004). A guide to more enlightened living.

James Redfield, *The Secret of Shambhala: In Search of the Eleventh Insight* (New York, NY: Warner Books, 1999). Presents many excellent principles of manifestation in story form.

Jane Roberts, *The Nature of Personal Reality: Specific and Practical Techniques for Solving Everyday Problems* (San Rafael, CA: Amber Allen Publishing, 1974).

Jane Roberts, *Seth Speaks: The Eternal Validity of the Soul* (San Rafael, CA: Amber Allen Publishing, 1972). The Seth books are the books rated most highly for expanding one's view of reality by the majority of explorers I have met over the decades, when I ask them "Which book has influenced your life the most" ?

ABOUT THE AUTHOR

Dr. Joseph Gallenberger is a clinical psychologist with thirty years experience as a therapist. In 1992 be began to investigate psychokinesis (PK), the ability to influence matter through non-physical means. PK can be used to illuminate light bulbs, bend metal and plastic, sprout seeds in your hand, influence computers, dice and slot machines, and create healing and abundance—all just using the power of your mind.

After achieving powerful PK results at a university laboratory, Dr. Gallenberger has used his discoveries to host over seventy Inner Vegas Adventures™, where his students achieve dramatic physical and psychological healing, strong influence over dice and slot machines, and many marvelous manifestations in their lives at home.

Dr. Gallenberger is a senior facilitator at The Monroe Institute and developed the Institute's highly successful MC² program which teaches psychokinesis, healing, and manifestation. Joe also developed SyncCreation®, a course in manifestation, which is the home study version of the MC² program. He is also the creator of four CD/downloads: *Manifesting with Hemi-Sync*, *Partner's Meditation*, *Liquid Luck*, and his latest, *Abundance Waterfall*.

His book, *Inner Vegas: Creating Miracles, Abundance and Health*, takes a wild ride into world of psychokinesis where mind, energized by the heart, influences matter. It reveals what is possible when we apply intention and heart-centered energy to mold reality to our desires.

In *Liquid Luck: The Good Fortune Handbook,* he explores the vital components for powerful abundance creation. His knowledge and the stories of other's success show us that we can indeed be miracle workers in our own lives, and find a clear path toward our dreams lit with humor and heart.

For more information visit Dr. Joseph Gallenberger's website: *www.SyncCreation.com.*

RELATED TITLES

If you enjoyed *Liquid Luck,* you may also enjoy other Rainbow Ridge titles. Read more about them at *www.rainbowridgebooks.com.*

Inner Vegas: Creating Miracles, Abundance, and Health
by Joe Gallenberger

God's Message to the World: You've Got Me All Wrong
by Neale Donald Walsch

*Dying to Know You: Proof of God
in the Near-Death Experience*
by P. M. H. Atwater

*Imagine Yourself Well: A Practical Guide to Using Visualization
To Improve Your Health and Your Life*
by Frank DeMarco

The Cosmic Internet: Explanations from the Other Side
by Frank DeMarco

Dance of the Electric Hummingbird
by Patricia Walker

*Consciousness: Bridging the Gap between Conventional Science
and the New Super Science of Quantum Mechanics*
by Eva Herr

Messiah's Handbook: Reminders for the Advanced Soul
by Richard Bach

When the Horses Whisper:
The Wisdom of Wise and Sentient Beings
by Rosalyn Berne

Channeling Harrison, Book 1
by David Young

God Within: The Day God's Train Stopped
by Patti Conklin

Lessons in Courage
by Bonnie Glass-Coffin and Oscar Miro-Quesada

Your Soul Remembers: Accessing Your
Past Lives through Soul Writing
by Joanne DiMaggio

The Healing Curve: A Catalyst to Consciousness
by Sara Chetkin

INNER VEGAS TESTIMONIALS

"Every one of us has an "Inner Vegas" wanting to bestow upon us a fabulous life. Joe has a proven track record of success stories, and now he is sharing his infinite wealth of knowledge and inspiration so that anyone and everyone can tap into the infinite creative power within, and choose to consciously create a fulfilling and rich life!"

— Charlotte McGinnis, author, *A Golf Course in Miracles*

"A casino in Las Vegas is not the first place that comes to mind when one considers exploring unconditional love, performing experiments in quantum physics, or pursuing spiritual self-exploration. However, *Inner Vegas* interweaves experiences from each of these areas, and more, as Dr. Joe Gallenberger guides the reader along a winding path of personal growth and the manifestation of abundance. I personally participated in several of Joe's "Vegas Adventures" and can testify to the truth of not only the stories told, but the approaches taught, as Joe offers the wisdom and knowledge gained from a lifetime of self-exploration and experiences in realms of the anomalous, psi, and the extraordinary. Buckle your seat belt as you start reading *Inner Vegas*, as the reality of the importance of the journey rather than the map or the destination becomes clear."

— J. Richard Madaus, Ph.D., author, *Think Logically, Live Intuitively: Seeking the Balance*

"Both practical and inspirational, *Inner Vegas* takes you on a journey of discovery of the true dimensions of human potential. Tracing his own baby steps through the psychic world of PK (psychokinesis) and manifesting, Dr. Gallenberger finds an unlikely ashram at the Las Vegas casinos, where he diligently works to gain insight and mastery of mind over matter. He offers the fruits of his personal search to readers and program participants alike. Many down to earth tips and exercises spark each of us to experience the magic of discovering our own latent abilities and talents. Fascinating stories illustrate mind-stretching truths that change the way one thinks about how the world really works. Truly a journey to higher consciousness amid the Vegas lights!"

—Carol Sabick delaHerran, executive director and president of The Monroe Institute

"This book is for everyone. All of us have to make decisions every day and I often second guess and doubt myself, because I'm worried that I'll do the "wrong" thing. Reading your book was a reminder for me to be open and awake to guidance, and to create and manifest what I desire to have in my life. And it works! When I pay attention to the principles that you teach, I am always surprised at the outcome—it's often even better than what I imagined. You offer practical and easy-to-use tips and techniques to polish the skill of manifestation that is within all of us! And, most of all, you make it fun!"

—Marinda Stopforth, residential facilitator, The Monroe Institute

Inner Vegas brings intuition, logic, and heart together, a magical formula for creating lasting abundance, inner confidence, and a new freedom to expand our horizons. Joe's principles work. I have accompanied him to the Vegas workshops and assisted in teaching his week-long courses for over ten years. As a result, I have witnessed countless 'miracles' of manifesting, healing, and PK that go beyond logic and move into the realm of the magical. *Inner Vegas* is uplifting, relevant and *liberating*.

—Patty Ray Avalon, author of *Inner States—Dawning of Awareness, The Creative Way* and *Positively Ageless with Hemi-Sync*

Rainbow Ridge Books publishes spiritual, metaphysical, and self-help titles, and is distributed by Square One Publishers in Garden City Park, New York.

To contact authors and editors, peruse our titles, and see submission guidelines, please visit our website at *www.rainbowridgebooks.com*.

For orders and catalogs, please call toll-free: (877) 900-BOOK.